32 REGRETS

Life's splendor forever lies in wait about each one of us in all its fullness, but veiled from view, deep down, invisible, far off. It is there, though, not hostile, not reluctant, not deaf. If you summon it by the right word, by its right name, it will come.

— FRANZ KAFKA, DIARIES, 1910–1923

CONTENTS

———

INTRODUCTION

———

All creators know that when they venture beyond the frontiers of the known, they can invent the extraordinary.

—DOM PERIGNON MARKETING CAMPAIGN

BEGINNINGS

I sat in the parking lot of an office park in a suburb of Columbus, Ohio, trying to talk myself into opening the car door. I dreaded having to get out and walk into work. *One foot in front of the other,* I told myself. But another part of my brain said, *Stay in the car, turn the key, back out of this spot, and go home.* As I sat there arguing with myself, I started to feel a bit like Cameron Frye in *Ferris Bueller's Day Off*: "I'll go, I'll go, I'll go, I'll go . . . shit."

My first job in corporate America came in the form of merchandising for Abercrombie & Fitch. I served as an assistant merchant, managing a team of designers based in Columbus working with factories in Vietnam and China to deliver clothing on time and on budget. The work sounds very creative, and in an *ideal* world it *would* be more creative, but I found myself facing the same few issues over and over. Generating new ideas to solve our problems was creative and fulfilling, but they were sometimes few and far between, which is exactly what you want in a business—steady progress.

While the designers created new styles and dreamed up new color schemes, graphic designers changed logos and logo placement, and technical designers drafted measurements and specifications on garment sizing. Merchandise planners told me when I needed to have orders land to get them into stores on time. Someone else cut the purchase orders. All that was left for me was to be the conduit through which information flowed from our headquarters to our factories in Vietnam and China.

As it turned out, I mostly argued over pricing, shipping method, and delivery dates via email. The lack of real ownership of the creative process led to a growing resentment and dread of having to go into the office. I knew I wasn't genuinely excited for this work and wanted to be in a more creative role, actually developing ideas and looking for new trends, but I wasn't sure how to make the transition. I began to look at entrepreneurs to see what projects were coming to life in the world around me, and I began to wonder if they were that much smarter or that much more business-savvy than I was. And I began a quest to find out.

But like any great twenty-three-year-old, I did not have much perspective on the world around me. So I left A&F without the knowledge I might have gained had I stayed. I wasn't sure where to go, so I moved back in with my mom and began looking for the next adventure.

I jumped from one job to the next, working at a ski resort and then leaving that place to work in sourcing and product development for a plastics manufacturing startup. Leaving that job, I decided that pursuing a master's degree in security studies would help me move into working in government. I achieved this master's, worked in federal consulting for a bit, and again felt the pull to start my own project.

While pursuing my master's, I received some funding to start a company to use drones for avalanche mitigation at ski resorts. I was slightly ahead of government regulations regarding the commercial use of drones and didn't recruit an adviser onto the project to help guide me. I traveled to conferences and worked on a business plan, but on a day to day basis, I really didn't know what I was doing or what I was supposed to be doing.

As a result, I failed completely to get a business set up. I didn't manage to commit to this idea and felt like a total failure. In working for myself from home, I didn't manage my time effectively and set unrealistic timelines for when each part of the project would be due. So I returned to working in government.

Working in government was a fantastic experience. I met some incredibly motivated, talented, and caring people, and I got to work on projects that impacted the agencies I spent time working for and consulting with. I, however, could not overcome the large sense of apathy and bureaucracy within the government; it didn't suit me. I grew tired with the layers of bureaucracy and red tape and became interested in tech and software companies for their agile, "wear many hats" versatility and the opportunity to work on multiple facets of the business.

I started to convince myself that working in a tech startup would be the answer. So I found a job with a software startup, which had freedom and autonomy for a young guy who wanted to learn and try and fail and wake up the next day to do it all over again. And, for a while, working in a startup was amazing. I got to help build strategies, develop business plans, and work with clients across industries. I found that, as the startup scaled, I was pulled in many different directions. At first, I was able to plan and prepare for client challenges. But as we scaled, the pace and intensity of problems scaled with us, and I was no longer able to create unique solutions to each problem—I simply had to react to each one as it came.

Eventually, reacting to client issues and meeting client demands took so much of my time and energy that I was exhausted at the end of each day. I had no motivation left to create for myself; I was simply drained.

As I worked and moved from job to job, I was excited with each new opportunity. Inevitably, I felt the guilt, shame, and pangs of regret for taking a new job rather than the time to invest in myself, figure out a course to travel, and give myself time and space for my own creative project.

Throughout the course of my career, I started journaling. I started writing every night to reflect on the day. I wanted to learn what gave me energy, what drained my energy, and where I felt like I could have improved or what one thing really stood out from my day. When I sat down to look at ten years' worth of journaling, I realized I had been talking about starting a business in one form or another.

In a 2017 journal entry, I wrote that "I am feeling like a failure for not having generated a profitable business idea yet. It seems like everyone else has a startup and profits coming in the door, but I just can't seem to find an idea. I'm still hung up on being outside and spending as much time in nature as possible."

In that moment I realized I was stalling on my own dreams. I learned so much from each new experience, but I had a nagging feeling that something was wrong with me. I felt that I wasn't smart enough, I couldn't commit fully to any work presented to me, I was never "both feet in." I never quite had the gumption, the fire, the feeling of being completely aligned with an organization's mission. In short, I was never fulfilled in working for others. And then, out of the blue, it hit me.

I had to take action and I had to start. It became clear through my journaling that I had been talking about starting a business in some nebulous form or another since 2008. I opened a Google Document, titled it "Thought Catalog," and began going through my journals and extracting all the business ideas I saw.

I had thirty-two ideas, ranging from a jiu-jitsu gi company, manufacturing and developing jiu-jitsu uniforms in unique colors and with unique graphic designs, to a hand-built bicycle company, making bespoke single-speed commuter and race bicycles and building a racing team around this premise. As I worked in HR consulting and with smaller companies, I began to dream of founding a consulting firm for startups looking to maintain their culture as they grow.

During this period of transition, in order to start unraveling the world of creative entrepreneurs, I began to read as many books and blogs as I could on entrepreneurship and personal development. Multiple entrepreneurs and personal growth gurus recommended journaling, writing about your day—what excited me, what drained me—and being able to use that writing to take stock over a period of time. So I began a habit of writing in a journal.

I was sporadic to say the least, but what I learned from writing over a period of ten years was astonishing.

REGRETTERS AND DREAMERS

I didn't have a list of thirty-two ideas of companies to start. I had a meticulously curated list of thirty-two regrets over ten years. Thirty-two companies I didn't start. Thirty-two companies I had never allowed to manifest fully in my mind. And when that realization flashed in my head, I decided that this failure to begin could never happen again.

I made a pact with myself that I would not end up with a thirty-third regret, and I theorized that we must have two types of people in this world: Dreamers and Regretters.

Dreamers pursue passion and chase it down, practicing divergent thinking and recognizing that the world has very few true boundaries; they recognize the limitless potential in our world.

Regretters, on the other hand, are in the same position I found myself in. Regretters predominantly practice convergent thinking. They don't know how to expand their concept of the world and instead spend time wishing, like I did, that they had started something years ago when they'd first had the idea.

At thirty-three years old, a decade after sitting in that first parking lot at Abercrombie & Fitch, I had sat in plenty more parking lots (some metaphorical) feeling the same way. I felt the dread, the anguish, the guilt and shame, and I knew I was better than this feeling of being stuck. I knew I needed to create something on my own. But I didn't, and I kept interviewing and taking other jobs, knowing that in six months I would find the new position's flaws as well, and I would again feel the pull to create.

WHY ME?

I always wanted to create something of my own. I realized I hadn't yet found an outlet for my creativity, a way to contribute, to be of value, and to let myself truly feel alive in the world. And so I set out on a journey to learn how to turn my future from one of regret into one of opportunity. I had to learn to become a Dreamer and then chase that dream relentlessly.

This book is simply a beginning for me. It started with some nervous calls and some really nervous interviews. But I was more curious to see where this journey would take me than I was afraid of failing. As soon as I had the first two interviews completed, I was hooked. I started researching more, I started looking for other creatives to interview, and I realized this process is what I have loved doing in my life. I became curious about something, so I chased down as much information as I could find about it.

As I got into the interviews and creating the stories, looking for commonalities, I was hooked. I knew that this was the type of creative work I had been looking for. As I commuted to work, as I worked out, or as I was doing anything else, my brain was always working on this book, this idea. I had found an outlet for my creativity and recognized the pattern in something I had been doing for a long time: research. I realized that my curiosity was my creativity. And I dove in.

I knew I had found something that allowed me to fulfill my interest, my dream, my passion. This book is just the beginning of the path for me. I realized I had other ideas, I had other content I wanted to produce, I had partners I wanted to approach about creative projects together. Beneath my list of thirty-two regrets was the underlying core: creating for myself and getting to share this information with others.

The creative process of writing this book got me curious. I wanted to know why Dreamers were different in their approach to creativity. I needed to know why. And this book has become a way for me to pursue my curiosity and engage with others and find freelance work in a way that makes me come alive through creativity. Speaking to the Dreamers for this book got me fired up. I had to step off a prescribed path and start building my own.

NOT ALONE AMONGST REGRETTERS

As I took a look at the world around me, I realized I wasn't alone in this battle. The Society for Human Resource Management (SHRM) in their "Employee Job Satisfaction and Engagement Survey" from 2017 found that "job satisfaction and employee engagement levels remain high; 89 percent of U.S. employees reported being somewhat or very satisfied with their current job role."[1] This statistic stopped me in my tracks as I let it sink in. I was initially skeptical of the number, and as I kept reading, I realized that 51 percent of people reported being satisfied to a somewhat lesser degree than the top 38 percent of respondents who were very satisfied with their current position.

I needed a few moments to fully understand what this data meant: 51 percent of people are only somewhat satisfied with their current position. Roughly half the people asked weren't

---

1   Christine Lee, Evren Esen, and Samantha DiNicola, "Executive Summary: Employee Job Satisfaction and Engagement: The Doors of Opportunity are Open" (Alexandria, 2017).

excited about their job, a notion that ran counter to everything I had been told about finding work that you love. This statistic told me I was not alone in not being excited to go to work every day. That means that this group also falls into the camp of regret.

In a study of 2,000 British adults, 40 percent said they regretted their life choices.[2] The biggest regret was spending too much time at work and not enough time traveling. With regret being such a powerful emotion, I realized that the opportunity still exists for us to become Dreamers. The amazing thing is that we have the power and the ability to make these changes. With creativity, we have the power to create a life we truly want to live.

With the outlook that the world is divided into camps of Regretters and Dreamers, I began to look at the world around me and search for creative entrepreneurs with qualities that would inspire me. I looked for:

- People who had taken their passion and successfully turned it into a business,
- How those same people achieved their goals,
- What skills I needed to cultivate to replicate their success, and
- Whether I needed to obtain a particular degree or pedigree to achieve my goals.

---

2   John Anderer, "Hindsight Is 20/20: 4 Out Of 10 Adults Regret Their Life Choices," Study Finds (Remember A Charity, July 23, 2019).

I had a limiting belief that I could never be a successful entrepreneur because I lacked a Master of Business Administration. I didn't have faith in my ideas; all of them were garbage.

Having spoken to over a dozen creative entrepreneurs, I quickly realized I was dead wrong.

INSPIRATIONS

As I started to write this book and looked through my list of thirty-two ideas, I realized each of these ideas, on its own, had merit. They may not have been the best of ideas, but perhaps when combined with other ones on the list or new ideas, there was certainly a viable business contained within this list. I was not lacking ideas. I was lacking creativity, and I needed to find a way to harness and enhance my own creativity in order to view this list with fresh eyes and find the connections to build the business.

This book was designed to help the "somewhat satisfied" within the 89 percent career-aged adults identified by the SHRM study with a concrete method to become a Dreamer, rather than a Regretter.[3] To accomplish that mission, I interviewed some of the most creative people I could think of who helped me feel inspired and compelled to create.

I interviewed Maximilian Büsser, founder of the watch brand Maximilian Büsser and Friends, to learn how fourteen years

---

3   Christine Lee, et.al., "Executive Summary: Employee Job Satisfaction and Engagement" (Alexandria, 2017).

working for other watch brands reviving their businesses had burnt him out and the passing of his father was his sign that he needed to create.[4] This realization jumpstarted his obsession with creation. Desperately needing to create for himself, Max quit his job rebooting and developing new product lines for existing watch brands. He spent two years working on the first sketch of his own watch in his apartment in Geneva. He didn't have any watchmakers, let alone a factory in which to produce his watches. Max fought to find production, called on friends to help him bring his sketches to life, and almost went bankrupt multiple times along the way.[5]

Fourteen years after creating that initial sketch, Max is still creating. His journey has been filled with trials and has almost led to bankruptcy four separate times. Max and his team have continuously found ways to overcome these trials, and he continues to produce only what he wants to see in the world: his very personal vision of what watchmaking should be.

I interviewed Ted Gushue, the founder of ERG Media, who holds a contract with Porsche Auto Group to manage its digital strategy. He also works with governments, tourism boards, and other clients seeking to improve their digital strategy. Ted didn't follow a specific plan to

4   SIHH2019: You Never Lose: You Win – Or You Learn / by MB&F, YouTube (MB&F, 2019).
5   SIHH2019: You Never Lose: You Win – Or You Learn / by MB&F, YouTube (MB&F, 2019).

get to where he is now; he followed his curiosity, letting his creativity forge a path, helping him to learn to take and edit better photos and putting together a convincing digital story and brand narrative. Ted decided to write his own story, and he has been creating ever since. His work focuses on the automobile, but he teaches us so much more about creating a life that is exactly the one you want to live every day.

As I interviewed these Dreamers, I realized that, like Max and Ted, they all enjoyed tremendous freedom. They were able to create their vision of what they wanted to see in the world, and they got to do it every day. They all had work experience in the arena they wanted to enter but brought their own perspective and still managed to dream and think of new ways to continue developing and challenging themselves and their idea.

What do creatives like Ted and Max do differently? Dr. George Land was one of the brains behind a 1968 NASA study to determine the most creative people to solve mission critical problems at NASA.[6] After developing the test for NASA, Land became curious about what happens to creativity from childhood into adulthood. Using the same test applied to NASA scientists, Land administered it to 1,600 children nationwide.[7] The findings were astounding.

---

6   Jim Rembach, "Innovation Secret Discovered at NASA," Beyond Morale: The Fearless Pursuit to Engage, October 31, 2016.

7   Coert Engels, "We Are Born Creative Geniuses and the Education System Dumbs Us down, According to NASA Scientists," Ideapod, 2018.

Of the 1,600 children tested, 98 percent of four- and five-year-olds scored in the highly creative range of the test, the top tier of creativity. Only 2 percent of the over 1 million adults sampled in this study fell into the highly creative range.[8]

This incredible drop in performance can be explained through multiple pathways. First, we start to develop a sense of self and ego and want to protect ourselves from hearing others proclaim, "That's a dumb idea." Second, our education system doesn't encourage divergent thinking; in fact, it encourages rote memorization and judging.[9]

But don't worry, the same NASA study found that the ability to create remains, but we seemingly put it off and forget about it, choosing logic and rationalizing instead of developing truly creative ideas and innovative solutions. Dr. Land defines this way of using imagination to create new ideas as *divergent thinking*, and every person on this planet can train that part of the brain and methodology of thinking. To do so, the process, Dr. Land suggests, is simple: You just have to dream.[10] Every time you pick up an object, think of ways to make it better. Every time you read an article, think of twenty different ways to write the hook for the story. The pathways to create divergent thinking are limitless. It just requires that we take one action: dream.

---

8   Engels, "We Are Born Creative Geniuses and the Education System Dumbs Us down, According to NASA Scientists."

9   *The Failure Of Success*, Dr. George Land, *YouTube* (TEDx, 2011).

10 *The Failure Of Success*, Dr. George Land, *YouTube* (TEDx, 2011).

BECOMING A DREAMER

This book is for anyone who has sat in the office parking lot trying to convince themselves to face another dreamless day. This book is for anyone who knows they have a creative dream, even if they cannot voice it out loud yet. This book is for the Dreamer who knows they have a vision to bring to life in the world but are not sure what first step to take.

In this book, you'll learn from watchmakers such as Maximilian Büsser and Kari Voutilainen about how they were never satisfied with what they saw in the industry and felt they needed to share their vision. Learn from Ted Gushue about creating your own path and never asking for permission. Learn from Sheena Lawrick, a Canadian Olympian, how never really fitting in helps you find your place. And learn from Dan Killian, my friend and funding winner from *Shark Tank* for his game Pricetitution, about how to remain creative, how to generate ideas, and how practicing can help you become creative.[11]

Dreamers embody the spirit of pushing beyond what we currently know to be true; without their rule-bending, paradigm-shifting ideas, life might just be very boring and analytical. They open new ways of thinking, not just for themselves, but for everyone around them. As a society and as individuals, we have an opportunity to create a world of Dreamers, who share the brightest part of ourselves with the world. We could live in a world where we continue to encourage high school and college graduates to pursue a traditional route of a career,

11   "Episode #10.19," *Shark Tank* (Culver City, California: ABC, April 14, 2019).

where "60 percent of millennials are currently open to a new job opportunity" live in a world where those 60 percent, who are constantly looking for the next new thing, find extremely rewarding work in creating a vision for their life and work and giving themselves permission to create.

Everyone has the potential to become a dreamer. We just need to become familiar with our curiosity, give ourselves permission, and identify what it is within ourselves that we most want to see alive and well in the world around us.

CHAPTER 1

DICHOTOMOUS WORLDS

———

AN INTRODUCTION TO CONVERGENT AND DIVERGENT THINKING

You can't use up creativity. The more you use the more you have.

—MAYA ANGELOU

I used to think I would have a moment of clarity when I learned exactly what I was supposed to be doing on this planet. It really never showed up. The truth is, if you wait for that moment, you are going to spend a lifetime waiting. The only thing you can do is the hardest thing to do: you just have to get started.

I started journaling in 2008, writing most nights to reflect on the day. I wanted to learn what gave me energy, what I was really supposed to be doing on this planet. A lot of pages are just lists and brain-mapping. I have pages filled with business ideas, maybe just a quick bullet point, maybe paragraphs. But the information was right in front of my face. When I sat down to look at ten years' worth of journaling, I realized I had been talking about starting a business in one form or another for the better part of a decade.

Ten years.

That is 3,650 days.

That is 87,600 hours.

Ten years is a long time to think about something and not take action, not make an honest effort at starting a business. Trust me, I know.

During this decade, I had times when I was fully engaged in the work I was doing and I wasn't thinking about starting a business. But at other times it was all I could think about, and I filled pages and pages of journals with the tormented words of someone who direly wanted to create but had no idea where to begin.

This regret is why I saved some money and quit my job at Abercrombie & Fitch. I thought taking some time off and working at a ski resort would provide that jolt of inspiration I needed to have an "aha" moment. From there, I jumped from one opportunity to the next, but I never really did the work of figuring out my actual goals for the future.

And that is when I realized I was stalling on my own dreams. And dreams became something that occupied my mind more and more. How would I transfer the ideas into a vision I wanted to bring into the world? This question became a subject of thought for me more and more, and my curiosity grew. So I started to think about how this world is constructed of the risk-takers and those who just follow the status quo.

As I jumped from job to job, I would be satisfied for a bit with the novelty of a new position, and when the novelty was gone I was still in the same place I had always been: a guy looking to start a company with no clear path to tread. I was a Regretter. I regretted switching jobs, continuing to hunt for novelty in someone else's dreams. I looked at colleagues who went on to create companies of their own and was in awe, but also jealous. They had dreams and were pursuing them. And I was still hunting for the next job and feeling the pull of my creativity.

In a 2015 journal entry, I wrote: "I keep asking myself what I really want to do—what's going to allow me to fully express my passion? What do I really, really love doing deep down in there? What will be intellectually stimulating? What in the hell is it?"[12] And I realized that maybe the answer wasn't buried deep down—maybe it was right in front of me. Perhaps I just needed to put one foot in front of the other and start living a path toward creativity.

---

12   Authors personal journals, December, 2015.

These experiences helped shape my vision that there are two groups of people on this planet: Regretters and Dreamers. Regretters and Dreamers are similar people—remember that 98 percent of kids scored as highly creative? Yup. Same concept—they all started with the same abilities. But what separates Dreamers and Regretters is their method of thinking and their ability to execute on their own dream. Regretters will give up at the first sign of resistance; Dreamers persist, chasing their own path and building it one day at a time.

HOW NASA GOT ITS GROOVE, ER, CREATIVITY BACK

Dr. George Land and Dr. Beth Jarman were contracted by NASA to help understand who the most creative folks within NASA were and assign them to work on the most challenging problems NASA had at that time. The test helped NASA accomplish its mission with even greater skill and precision and led Land and Jarman to wonder where creativity really derived from and what this meant for the greater population.

In 1968, they began a longitudinal study of creativity, planning to test 1,600 children at ages five, ten, fifteen, and then later testing a group of adults to determine the changes in creativity over time.[13] At age five, 98 percent of study participants scored in the highly creative range. At ten years old, that creativity diminishes, and only 30 percent of ten-year-olds scored in the highly creative range. By fifteen

---

13   Larry A Vint, "Fresh Thinking Drives Creativity & Innovation," *QUICK - Journal of the Queensland Society for Information Technology in Education* 2005, no. 94 (2005): pp. 20-22.

years old, only 12 percent of study participants scored in the highly creative range.[14] And with a sample size of over 1 million adults, with an average age of thirty-one years old, the study found that only 2 percent of the adults tested scored in the highly creative range.[15]

Age Group Tested	Number Tested	Percent who scored in the "highly creative" range
5 Years Old	1,600	98 percent
10 Years Old	1,600	30 percent
15 Years Old	1,600	12 percent
25+ Years Old	280,000	2 percent

Table 1: The Changes in Creativity Discovered by Land & Jarman's Longitudinal Study[16]

I was blown away by the fact that only 2 percent of adults scored in the highly creative category, and I wanted to understand why. Evidently, within the camps of Dreamers and Regretters, Dreamers make up only 2 percent of the population, and while I do not think 98 percent of people are Regretters, I am assuming that a large portion of that 98 percent feels unfulfilled and stuck in trying to launch a creative project.

Armed with those definitions, what did Land and Jarman learn from their work with NASA? Dr. Land points out in his TEDx Tucson talk, "The idea emerged that we still don't know where creativity comes from. Is it that some people

---

14   Vint, "Fresh Thinking Drives Creativity & Innovation," p.20.
15   *The Failure Of Success*, Dr. George Land, *YouTube* (TEDx, 2011).
16   Vint, "Fresh Thinking Drives Creativity & Innovation p.20.

are born with it and others are not? Or is it learned—does it come from our experience in life?"[17] Most people are born with the innate ability to create.

The science behind this study focuses on the two types of thinking available to humans: convergent thinking and divergent thinking. Merriam-Webster dictionary defines convergent thinking as "thinking (as in answering a multiple-choice question) that weighs alternatives within an existing construct or model in solving a problem or answering a question to find one best solution and that is measured by IQ tests." This kind is thinking that involves judging, reviewing, and dismissing ideas in pursuit of the best solution. In short, convergent thinking is all about analytical, rational thought.

Merriam-Webster defines divergent thinking as "creative thinking that may follow many lines of thought and tends to generate new and original solutions to problems," and divergent thinking is about idea generation, blue-sky "what if?" thinking.

Phil Charron, executive vice president of Think Company, does a good job applying these dictionary definitions to our real life. He defines convergent thinking as "the practice of trying to solve a discrete challenge quickly and efficiently by selecting the optimal solution from a finite set."[18] He defines divergent thinking, on the other hand, as "taking a challenge and attempting to identify all of the possible

---

17   *The Failure Of Success*, Dr. George Land, *YouTube* (TEDx, 2011).

18   Phil Charron, "Divergent Thinking vs Convergent Thinking," Think Company (Think Company, March 12, 2019).

drivers of that challenge, then listing all of the ways those drivers can be addressed."[19]

In his TEDx Tucson talk, Dr. Land uses an analogy that is key to these paradigms of thinking: convergent thinking is like a brake on a car, and divergent thinking is like an accelerator. Doing each task separately makes each possible, but doing both at the same time actually causes a severe reduction in our brain's ability to do either well. Dr. Land used MRI to study the brain, and when asked to complete convergent and divergent thinking at the same time, the brain's power was greatly reduced, and neurons were actually fighting each other for capacity within our brains.[20]

FROM DEFINITION TO DEFINING MOMENT
Once I heard these definitions, I identified this area as the single major difference between Regretters and Dreamers. Regretters practiced predominantly convergent thinking, looking at exactly why an idea would never work and suffering from analysis paralysis, while Dreamers practiced a fair amount of divergent thinking, then filtered that thinking through convergent thinking to arrive at the right solution for their specific problem or desired end state.

When I sorted this distinguishing factor out, I quickly realized I was in the camp of Regretters, as someone who had told myself that my ideas were stupid, or quickly disqualified them as not good enough. When I was given grant funding in graduate

---

19 Charron, "Divergent Thinking vs Convergent Thinking."
20 *The Failure Of Success*, Dr. George Land, *YouTube* (TEDx, 2011).

school to pursue researching the use of drones for avalanche mitigation, I thought I had actually moved from the world of Regretters to Dreamers.

When I started my research, I didn't have a business plan, and I didn't have a strategy for what I was going to do during my summer research, aside from studying avalanche conditions and finding a drone system that I could bolt cameras and avalanche mitigation tools onto. I had a plan for getting the business going, but I didn't have a plan on how to research, what my daily structure would look like, or how I would continue to approach the work.

After not working hard enough in grad school to really chase my drone company, I gave up on my ability to start a business and began hopping between jobs and looking for something that would provide meaningful work. In my failure to structure the work I needed to do into smaller pieces, I failed to have a plan to build a business. Being twenty-seven-years-old at the time, I thought that the pieces would become self-evident and easy to organize once I was going.

CONVERGENT AND DIVERGENT THINKING APPLIED

In failing to launch my drone business, I started to wonder what was actually preventing me from launching. As I look back on it, I could give a million excuses. What went through my head was more of a litany of reasons why the company would fail, why the product wouldn't work, and why using drones in harsh environments just wasn't a reality of the current state.

What I did was weigh my idea against the current method of how avalanche mitigation and avalanche victim rescue is conducted. I started with an expectation that I had to be head and shoulders above the current way of doing it, and that seemed insurmountable. In my head, I started to convince myself the idea was stupid. And in turn, I worked less and less on the project because my thinking told me that using drones for avalanche control and victim recovery would never work. And I brought that thought into existence.

I avoided taking the risk because I was stuck in the ways of convergent thinking. I wasn't taking the risk that this method was the future. I was a Regretter. And to become a Dreamer I had to radically change my thinking and explore what it meant to look at the world through the eyes of a divergent thinker.

A MOVE TOWARD SELF-EMPLOYMENT: THERE ARE DREAMERS OUT THERE

During our interview, Sheena Lawrick asked me point blank: "Why would you live by someone else's rules?" She continued, explaining that living within the confines of a traditional work role was not a life in which she was interested. She wanted to work, but also to live her life and pursue the activities she wanted when she wanted to. I was intrigued by this statement. I wanted to know, aside from SHRM, what other information was out there that might help me to understand the gravity of the situation.

I turned to FreshBooks' "Second Annual Self-Employment Report" to learn what the future holds for self-employment in the United States. Its research supports that there exists the potential for "27 million Americans to leave the corporate world in favor of self-employment by 2020, bringing the total number of self-employed Americans to 42 million."[21]

The trend is moving toward the direction of self-employment as Sheena proposes. FreshBooks found that "Self-employed professionals overall enjoy more career satisfaction than those with traditional jobs (71 percent vs. 61 percent). This satisfaction gap grows with age as the majority of self-employed professionals realize one or more of the following: more work life balance, better health, higher incomes."[22]

So if 71 percent of people are more satisfied being self-employed, I definitely needed to become a Dreamer, and turn idea number thirty-three into something I would not regret moving forward with. Armed with the knowledge of convergent and divergent thinking, I became aware of my thoughts, what camp they might fall in, and whether or not they were helping me advance or destroying my creativity and stifling my ability to grow, ideate, and move forward.

We may need time to unwind some of the teachings of our childhoods, and we may have to be willing to sacrifice some

21 Christine Lee, et.al., "Executive Summary: Employee Job Satisfaction and Engagement" (Alexandria, 2017).

22 Carly Moulton and Dave Cosgrave, "Second Annual Self-Employment Report," FreshBooks (FreshBooks Cloud Accounting, April 2018).

of our own beliefs to improve the quality of our lives and reclaim our creative genius. To do so, we have to understand how we created a world of Regretters, what we need to do to combat that world, and how to change our outlook to create more Dreamers.

CHAPTER 2

CREATING A WORLD OF REGRETTERS

A man is not old until regrets take the place of dreams.

—JOHN BERRYMORE

As you may recall, Dr. Land and Dr. Jarman's study on creativity found that only 2 percent of adults scored in the "highly creative" range. They had a number of theories as to why this result happened and what caused this shift, and what they found was shocking.

Looking at the history of humankind, Dr. George Land realized that specific periods of history contributed directly to developing or hindering our creativity. In his TEDx Tucson talk, Dr. Land points out that one of the major inflection points in human advancement was the development of science and the idea of replicable experimentation. Land argues that this discovery allowed humanity to build and scale processes and repeat scientific experiments, leading directly to the rise of manufacturing. Land explains that with the rise of manufacturing processes and the development and building of factories, "we had to build factories for human beings, too, called schools. So we could manufacture people who could work well in the factories."[23]

With school primarily focusing on developing humans to support work in factories, creativity was not necessarily part of the core curriculum. Dr. Land's theory is that industrialization and the rise of automation "has produced so much progress, that we have now turned success into failure."[24] His argument is that in pushing industrialization so far and succeeding beyond our wildest imaginations in the interconnected globalized climate we live in, we have created a world of "turbulent, unpredictable change."[25]

In the current world, the old system of using school as a system to educate factory workers completing rote tasks is no longer relevant. Dr. Land's argues that to succeed in the current chaotic times, we must create a world of innovators who can rise to the challenge, peek over the horizon, and see the future.[26] Then set to creating that future.

---

23 *The Failure Of Success*, Dr. George Land, *YouTube* (TEDx, 2011).
24 *The Failure Of Success*, Dr. George Land, *YouTube* (TEDx, 2011).
25 *The Failure Of Success*, Dr. George Land, *YouTube* (TEDx, 2011).
26 *The Failure Of Success*, Dr. George Land, *YouTube* (TEDx, 2011).

UNDERSTANDING REGRET

The Cambridge English Dictionary defines regret as a verb meaning "to feel sorry or unhappy about something you did or were unable to do." Merriam Webster adds that regret is "to mourn the loss or death, to miss very much, or to be sorry for." I believe these definitions cover the very core of what it is to live life as a Regretter. You live with a feeling of loss and mourn the ideas you had upon which you never acted. And I would argue this area is one in which we have created a disengaged global workforce, forced to pursue the path of regret rather than empowered to take the path of the dreamer.

One of the most painful features of creating a world of Regretters is the way regret shapes our future behavior. Dan Cumberland has researched the impact, finding that "psychologically the way you consider your past is the way you imagine your future. If you allow yourself to live in a paradigm of regret—where harsh voices condemn you for your mistakes and curse your attempts to step into the unknown—you will lack the ability to imagine an open and hopeful future. This is why the psychology of regret can be so harmful—the regrets of your past instill fear of the unknown in your future."[27]

That fear of failure in the future prevents so many of us from taking on creative and challenging work, and making a decision to take a leap of faith in yourself. It's helpful to take a step back and look at all the skills and experiences you have to remind yourself that you do have the capability and are

---

27   Dan Cumberland, "The Psychology of Regret and How to Overcome It," The Meaning Movement, June 20, 2016.

uniquely positioned for whatever creative project exists in your mind.

Cumberland's research found that, by focusing on regret, "instead of the enormous possibility of what you could do or create, you are walking into a future full of land mines and booby traps. The only way to clear space for possibility is to first find freedom for yourself in your stories."[28]

You may find it helpful to examine the thoughts, limiting beliefs, and reasons you are not pursuing your creative work to understand what limiting beliefs are holding you back from being successful. By noticing them when they arise, you can begin to decide if they serve you or not, and if they are no longer serving you, you need to have a paradigm shift and reset your thinking. Owning your stories, your past failures—real or perceived—acknowledging them, and then being able to decide whether they are real or perceived allows you to take that initial step forward to bringing your creativity alive.

HOW WE CREATED REGRETTERS

We have created a system of Regretters using a variety of methods. In my own experience, I never really found core curriculum items at school to be terribly engaging. I worked hard because I wanted to be rewarded with good grades but had no impetus in receiving good grades to focus on creative work.

---

28 Cumberland, "The Psychology of Regret and How to Overcome It."

From a young age I learned that the curriculum of math, science, English, and a foreign language was the core to what we needed to learn. Classes like art, woodshop, and physical education were secondary to learning how to do simple math or the basics of grammar.

Relegating art, music, shop, and physical education classes to a lower priority has diminished the quality of divergent thinking that students do. These are classes where I can see a clear tie-in to core values of generating novel ideas through creative thinking. This diminished importance in the curriculum leads me to believe that schools are reducing methods by which students apply convergent and divergent thinking separately.

My experience was that I could get through school by memorizing formulas in math and science and committing to memory vocabulary words and their spellings for foreign language tests only to quickly forget them. I often found that shifting out of that pattern of memorization, like knowing chemical equations and how to find the area under a curve, enabled me to actually retain that information better. And I learned better by having time to work on a sculpture in art class or a project in the wood shop.

Why? I was letting my brain slip out of convergent thinking mode. I was no longer analyzing a problem, judging a solution, and dismissing others; I was engaged in divergent thinking, looking for new ways to complete a sculpture, new ways to give it meaning, or learning new ways to create a table from a pile of wood. I was thinking about new ideas and possibilities, and that helped me to solidify my own knowledge of the core material I was supposed to learn.

Learning by rote memorization had a lasting impact on me—I was good at it, but I wasn't sure I enjoyed the process, or actually truly retained information, or found novel ways to complete the work assigned to me. I tremendously enjoyed photography, woodshop, and creative writing, but I never felt compelled to excel at classes in which rote memorization was required. I knew that I liked creating something new, especially working with my hands, and not repeating information for the sake of memorizing it—leaving a lasting impact on me.

SKIPPING SCHOOL

Some of the creatives I spoke to skipped school to pursue their passion, and I would argue they are some of the most free-thinking and creative people on the planet. Like Tim Bent, the owner and founder of Bentley's London, a specialist vintage shop Tim founded in 1989.

Tim Bent is the quintessential British gentleman. That is to say, Tim Bent is the quintessential British gent, if that gent had a good bit of punk rocker and a rebellious streak in him. Tim speaks to me from his shop in the Pimlico Design District on Lower Sloane Street in London, with a measured cadence that makes you want to lean in and listen closer. Tim chooses his words in what seems a careful but breezy manner, and you can almost picture him staring into a gin and tonic, giving it a carefree stir as he speaks. Tim's melodic British accent comes to life as he talks about his work in building Bentley's, with his namesake store supplying vintage leather goods, trunks, luggage, and Edwardian accessories to the modern collector.

Tim's "entrepreneurial spirit started pretty young, and grew from clothes into accessories, and Edwardian accessories, and the luggage was a very natural next step." While in school, Tim became interested in fashion and the ever-changing look of the classic British gentleman—the pressed slacks, tweed jacket, and Oxford shirt—and saw somewhat of an erosion of this look as Italian tailors took up the flag and brought the style forward in a more updated, modern fashion. Tim enjoyed this look tremendously, purchasing vintage tweed jackets and other clothing items and wearing them or often selling them to classmates to fund the next piece. While in sixth form, the British equivalent of U.S. high school, Tim decided he wanted to forego university and pursue his vintage resale business.

It was at this time that Tim had discovered vintage leather goods, such as a suitcases, briefcases, and steamer trunks. He found the quality of these vintage items from the early twentieth century astonishing and unlike anything he could currently find in the world of fast fashion and manufacturing. Tim was finding out that "people appreciate exemplary craftsmanship and that is very, very difficult to find now." In essence, Tim was providing a service in unique items that were well crafted, where the craft may no longer be alive or the cost so prohibitive that vintage was a good way to find something that would work.

Instead of completing his university degree, which likely would not have added to the skills Tim needed to attain success, Tim spoke with his parents, who were also in retail, and they fully supported his dream. Tim found a unique business that he enjoyed building, even though the initial market was small. Tim said, "I am doing what I like and just wait to find people that like it as well." Tim had patience. Tim also had resilience. He received a lot of "no"s in those first years of walking into stores and asking if they wanted some vintage pieces to complement their store.

Having an entrepreneurial spirit and having experienced firsthand at a young age what being an entrepreneur meant, Tim was hooked. He realized that formal education would no longer support his growth trajectory, and he would need to focus on developing his business and his brand on his own full time, rather than attend school and work part time. And this decision was the best Tim could have made, as he learned very quickly how to complete sales, how to find and source the vintage pieces that fueled his business, and the necessary skills to be successful and develop expertise in his field from firsthand experience.

Tim's ability to see the growth trajectory and his willingness to knock on shop doors and ask if store owners would like a consultation or some vintage pieces to tie the look of their store together proved a great learning lesson for him in divergent thinking: he would visualize a piece and his customer, buy things that would suit their needs, and develop patience to wait for his customers to find him.

The lessons learned in building his business taught Tim more than he might have learned in a school curriculum, allowing him the freedom to pursue and build his vision without needing to memorize facts and formulas that would not serve his business.

With that freedom is the cost, and privilege, of working for himself, and a satisfaction at the end of the day that he himself built the business. Tim stays motivated and hungry, having a hard time staying in the present moment. He is always looking to the future and thinking about the next piece. "I have this great Victorian sign, and we still use it as our motto, and it just says, 'The best is good enough.' And I think that's a very good driver to continue to remind myself of that—always keep looking for the best." Sometimes our best is not good enough, but trying and working hard toward your goals with self-belief and resilience will allow you to bring your own creative vision into the world.

BECOMING YOUR FIVE-YEAR-OLD SELF

In school, we learn to come up with new ideas and then immediately evaluate them for worth or merit. We try to switch our brain directly from divergent thinking into convergent thinking mode, causing the brain to fight itself for capacity. So, what's the solution? How do we regain the ability to score in the 98 percent of creative geniuses like our former five-year-old selves? We clearly cannot continue the education model created by the industrial revolution; the rapid pace of technological change needs to be matched by an education system that emphasizes creative thinking, novel idea generation, and rapid innovation.

Creating Regretters in a world of rapid technological innovation was easy. But ease will no longer suffice. Doing things the way we have always done them is the antithesis of innovation. In the world of Amazon, Apple, Facebook, Google, Microsoft, and Netflix, we can hardly imagine we are a society that does not reward creativity. Often we reward the wrong things—people who can memorize the formulas and learn the materials only as they will be presented on the test, not applying them in novel ways.

What we need in the world are people willing to question convention, people willing to find, nurture, and unleash their inner five-year-old on the challenges facing us today. We need creators who create for the sake of creation itself, to please only themselves. That organic nature of the development of creativity is what helps them sell their vision to the world. But we also need to understand the psychology and fear and regret, and how, if we are not careful, we can get stuck in that cycle of fear and regret and diminish the importance of our creative ideas and abilities.

Dr. Land understood something from his research that will benefit anyone reading this book—we all possess an incredibly powerful tool for generating creative, innovative ideas: our brain.[29] And the best part is that no two brains are exactly the same. Each of us with our own unique skills, background,

---

29   *The Failure Of Success*, Dr. George Land, *YouTube* (TEDx, 2011).

education, and experiences is able to generate novel ideas every day. The caveat is that each person individually has to decide what they are going to do with the power trapped in their brains. If you doesn't act on the instincts and ideas in your brain, you'll get a sinking feeling of regret for not taking action on an idea when it is first hatched.

CHAPTER 3

PSYCHOLOGY OF FEAR AND REGRET

I know that if I failed I wouldn't regret that, but I knew one thing I might regret is not trying.

—JEFF BEZOS

While thinking of starting some of these thirty-two businesses, I was terrified of failing. I felt like I was the only person in the world standing on the precipice looking into the abyss, and that I was the only one in this unique position. What I learned from speaking to friends and creative entrepreneurs was illuminating.

While interviewing creative entrepreneurs and looking at workplace satisfaction data, I saw that most people experience some form of fear or regret in their career. I believe that the most underlying fear for any creative who hasn't taken the leap is the simple fear of failure.

What about the fear of failure is so pervasive and so paralyzing? Maybe conditioning from school has taught us to fear, as getting an "F" on a test meant you weren't good enough.

This idea of fearing failure requires a perspective shift to really accomplish something special and to turn a passion into a business. I had to rewrite the narrative that potrays failure as a bad thing. Failing is a recognition and opportunity to learn. If I fail, plenty of other jobs are available in software sales or consulting. I know I have skills I can fall back on.

What's the worst that can happen? You may have to take a step back and return to a job or find a similar job and rebuild your plan. You may gain a new hobby, discover something new about yourself, learn about something you don't like to do, or more critically, learn about something that sets your soul on fire.

TURNING FEAR INTO YOUR MOST POWERFUL ALLY

Dan Killian speaks methodically and chooses his words with precision. Years of improv comedy have honed his ability to listen to a conversation for the smallest clue, and he is incredibly quick to crack a joke or catch onto an idea someone has laid out. As Dan talks, I can already hear him looking for his next idea. Dan and I discuss creative work and the regret that sometimes gets attached to such work.

Dan is the creator of the game Pricetitution, a game designed to make you argue pointlessly with your friends about how much money they would need to be paid to do silly things. Dan loved the process of building a game, but particularly loved that the game is really a veiled opportunity to help people connect on a deeper level.

Working at an advertising agency directly out of school, Dan knew he was on the wrong path. In our interview, Dan told me: "I went into advertising and seemed like the best fit to mix both worlds. And I specifically ended up going into that job on the account side, which is more of the business side. There were different teams that just did the creative side of things. And that was not the role that I was in. When I sent my dad an email, maybe six months into the job, and I was like 'I think I'm in the wrong department.'"

I asked Dan what it means to him to take on creative work. I posit that to be creative, if you have become a Regretter, you have to get to a point where you are fed up with your own storyline and telling yourself why you can't do something. This feeling manifests itself as discomfort and anger and resentment about your own inability to do something creative that starts to become so frustrating.

Dan responds that he worked outside of his chain of command but was afraid to make a jump to the creative side of the business. "I think it was just a fear that I didn't want to make the jump over, to make the transition over. I never made the leap but I always tried to. I took a creative copywriting class, I used to submit billboards, headlines, tag-lines. . . . I ended up getting a billboard at Wrigley Field for Miller Lite."

During this time, Dan admits he was working against himself and turning into a Regretter. "I was so frustrated with myself for not committing to something that I literally just decided, 'I'm going to make something and I have no idea what that is. But I'm going to make it and I'm going to do it. And I don't care what it is.'"

Dan thought up the idea for Pricetitution after a conversation with a friend. Dan found working on the game to be absolutely freeing. He felt as though he had a path forward, knew what he needed to do, and was able to move on from the frustration and the feeling of lacking free will. To build on his momentum, Dan booked a conference room every night at work and stayed from 6 to 9 p.m. to work on developing his game, honing ideas, and testing the game on coworkers.

Dan then started rapidly prototyping his game, going to bars with games and asking patrons to play early iterations of Pricetitution, allowing him insight into how the game was played and how long it kept players engaged. Pleasantly surprised with his results, Dan put the game into production, launched a Kickstarter, and recently received investment on NBC's *Shark Tank*.

EFFECTS OF REGRET
Dan overcame his fear regarding whether he could be successful on his own, allowing him to put to rest any regrets about being able to create his own business.

As it turns out, research supports that people tend to feel more regret when they have a choice in the matter, which makes it incredibly important to go out into the world and try to bring your vision to life. Researchers Marcel Zeelenberg, Wilco W. van Dijk, Antony S.R. Manstead, and Joop van der Pligt point out in their work "On bad decisions and disconfirmed expectancies: The psychology of regret and disappointment" that there are differences between regret and disappointment. One key takeaway is that regret is experienced when the outcome of a decision is in your own hands—when you have the opportunity to make a choice and you don't.[30]

This study found that "negative emotions often result when our current state of affairs is worse than initially expected. . . . This is the case when we chose a certain course of action because we expected it to be the best, but it turned out that another course of action would have been better. Following these 'bad decisions,' we are likely to experience regret."[31]

This point is where Dan found himself when he started on the account side of advertising. This is where I've found myself when I have tried to start work on a creative pursuit: I know that choosing not to exercise my own creativity and make a choice to commit to, and start, a business had led me to feel regret on more than one occasion because the choice was entirely mine. This is the world of Regretters.

---

30 Marcel Zeelenberg et al., "On Bad Decisions and Disconfirmed Expectancies: The Psychology of Regret and Disappointment," Cognition and Emotion 14, no. 4 (2000): pp. 521-541.

31 Marcel Zeelenberg et al., "On Bad Decisions and Disconfirmed Expectancies: The Psychology of Regret and Disappointment," p. 522.

Zeelenberg et al's study goes on to point out the aftereffects of regret. "Because the experience of regret involves the tendency to kick oneself, the tendency to correct one's mistake, and the motivation to undo the event, experienced regret should be associated with active attempts to undo the unpleasant effects of the decisions that went wrong."[32] Our subconscious brain recognizes the regret and pain, and to avoid that feeling again, our brain prevents us from taking a decisive action to step into the world of Dreamers.

Thus we will talk ourselves out of anything, out of starting a new project, out of attempting self-expression through a new form of art; our brain will prevent us from getting hurt. So, if we fail once and feel the sting of regret, and are presented with another opportunity to begin again, that initial failure enhances our fear of failure and negatively influences our ability to commit and try again.

I experienced this phenomenon when I received summer grant funding to explore using drones for avalanche mitigation. I built a business plan, I spoke to experts, I attended trade shows. I collected a lot of information but executed on none of it. I could have been on Capitol Hill lobbying for legislative change and regulatory changes around drones, but I didn't know what was next. I was paralyzed with fear about having to decide and overcommitting only to find out that regulation would never change.

32　Marcel Zeelenberg et al., "On Bad Decisions and Disconfirmed Expectancies: The Psychology of Regret and Disappointment," p. 526.

In hindsight, I know now all the steps I could have taken to push the ball forward, and I have learned from some of the best creative minds about how they might have solved some of these challenges. But in the moment, I personally failed. And I have since successfully avoided, or talked myself out of, starting any new venture to protect myself from that feeling of failure, and even the simple fear of failure.

OVERCOMING REGRET

Unlike me, Sheena Lawrick, a two-time Canadian Olympian, did not let fear of failure or regret drive her life. Following her Olympic career, Sheena coached at the university level at a CrossFit gym in Chicago and fell in love with coaching and working directly with clients on nutrition. When starting her company, Beyond the Box Nutrition, Sheena had no idea that she could start a company but had a belief that she should jump into entrepreneurship and not wait for permission.

When she left her full-time coaching job, a former client asked Sheena if she would be interested in starting a nutrition coaching business, and Sheena jumped. In two weeks, they had a website, plans, and a business model they knew could work.

Sheena never let regret or fear of failure stop her. In our interview she tells me that she's "never understood living in these boxes that people think they have to be in, right, like eight-five job, or Monday to Friday. I want to work when I want to work. And I also want to live my life." So Sheena was all in on Beyond the Box Nutrition.

She was also realistic in her approach, knowing that "there's going to be heartaches; there's going to be things that don't work out. But, to me, the alternative of staying stuck and staying in a place where you're like, 'If nothing changes, nothing changes.' That is the very definition of hell to me."

And Sheena hit the nail on the head. If nothing changes, nothing changes. We all fear failure, but if you go out and try, and worst-case scenario you fail, you aren't necessarily worse off than you are now. For one, you will have tried. Second, you will have learned multiple things about yourself, how you work, and whether that was the right business for you to try and get into. And worst-case scenario, you will resume working at a job similar to the one you have now until you find the next idea, but you simply have to try.

Sheena really eloquently summed up her entrepreneurial experience at the end of our conversation: "It comes down to a series of choices. And sometimes you can talk yourself out of anything, or you can talk yourself into anything. And at the end of the day, it just comes down to: one day, you're gonna have to make a choice. Otherwise, you're just wasting time." And so we find ourselves wasting time. Sometimes you just have to step up and decide to start moving toward the creativity you have been putting off.

ALL TOO COMMON

Research conducted by Susan B. Shimanoff in 1984 found regret to be the second most frequently named emotion in a study of the use of emotions in everyday language.[33] Second. Think about that for a moment. The fact that regret was the second most commonly expressed emotion should tell you everything you need to know: we live in a world inhabited by Regretters and now more than ever you must dive into your creativity and bring that vision to life.

As I reflect on that, I think about the regret I experienced sitting at a desk at a new company, six months after leaving my last job, wondering what could have happened had I taken the leap six months ago, and how far I might be along the journey to creative entrepreneurship. In "The Experience of Regret and Disappointment," Marcel Zeelenberg, Wilco W. van Dijk, Antony S.R. Manstead, and Joop van der Pligt look at the emotion of regret to understand what regret really is.

These researchers try to differentiate between regret and disappointment, offering that "regret arises from comparing an obtained outcome with a better outcome that might have occurred had a different choice been made," while "disappointment arises from comparing an obtained outcome with a better outcome that might have resulted from the same choice being made."[34]

33 Susan B. Shimanoff, "Commonly Named Emotions in Everyday Conversations," *Perceptual and Motor Skills 58*, no. 2 (April 1984): pp. 514-514.

34 Marcel Zeelenberg et al., "The Experience of Regret and Disappointment," *Cognition and Emotion* 12, no. 2 (1998): p. 222.

I found that, to find satisfaction, you must try your hand at a creative project to determine if it is the path you want to follow. Colleen Saffrey, Amy Summerville, and Neil J. Roese write in "Praise for regret: People value regret above other negative emotions" that "Individuals who ruminate on their regrets are more likely to report reduced life satisfaction and to experience difficulty coping with negative life events."[35]

I know this feeling of dwelling on regret and can attest to its real and raw power. And this research is all the more reason to dive in and try your hand at a creative project. On the other hand, by focusing on positive outcomes, you may enhance your outlook. Shifting our focus from regret to the creative future in store for us will positively impact our ability to bring a creative project to life.

THERE IS HOPE!
While regret, limiting beliefs, and the stories we tell ourselves can evidently influence us and hold us back, this loop prevents us from truly becoming a Dreamer. Fear and regret can cause major heartaches for people, not just in preventing them from taking action, but choosing a course of inaction can have damaging results on the long-term outlook for their future.

In section two of this book, we will learn from some of the world's most creative people to understand how they

---

35 Saffrey, Colleen, Amy Summerville, and Neal J. Roese. "Praise for Regret: People Value Regret above Other Negative Emotions." *Motivation and Emotion* 32, no. 1 (2008): 46–54.

overcame their fears and limiting beliefs to become a future version of their self. In section two, we will learn how these Dreamers moved beyond self-doubt, became immune to the sting of regret, and unleashed their creativity to bring their vision to life.

CHAPTER 4

DREAMERS: TODAY'S SUCCESS STORIES

The most difficult thing is the decision to act, the rest is merely tenacity. The fears are paper tigers. You can do anything you decide to do. You can act to change and control your life; and the procedure, the process is its own reward.

—AMELIA EARHART

When I started this project, I wanted to discover what made these creative entrepreneurs different from me. What became clear to me, as I spoke to more Dreamers, is that they are the epitome of the Ursula K. Le Guin quote, "A creative adult is a child who survived." Dreamers are the perfect group to remind us of what Dr. George Land found in his longitudinal study: five-year-olds are 98 percent highly creative.[36] And Dreamers have found a way to reclaim their

---

36 *The Failure Of Success*, Dr. George Land, *YouTube* (TEDx, 2011).

inner five-year-old and use it to build brands with unique outlooks in very different fields.

Their approach to work, their life, and even their outlook on life was very different to mine, and I wanted to know why. I wanted to learn from these Dreamers and understand their path so I could pick and choose the areas to emulate.

Dreamers are the people who learned from a young age to be creative. They may have worked in other fields, gained experiences unrelated to their current work, and found their way back to their own work. In some cases, they started creating and never stopped. I found that Dreamers, by and large, relentlessly fixate on their work, improving it, developing it, and thinking about what a future iteration of themselves will produce in the world. They chase their creativity from one opportunity to the next.

WHAT IS A DREAMER?

Merriam-Webster defines a Dreamer as "one who lives in a world of fancy and imagination; one who has ideas or conceives projects regarded as impractical: VISIONARY." Visionary is then defined as "having or marked by foresight and imagination." While I find both these definitions to be true for the creatives interviewed in this book, the one component that appears in both definitions is "imagination." Not only are Dreamers creative, but they have honed their imagination to their pursuit.

They have spent time developing their ethos, their style, their signature, and then executing a plan to follow the path they know they need to follow. While that process sounds simple, these creatives have found a way to leverage their imaginations to actually propel that journey and to add an additional sense of wonder to their creative projects and make them seem larger than life. It is the X-factor of imagination that Max brings to the table and that the most successful creatives have today. Their advantage is not just that they are creative, but that they have used their creativity to find a new way to combine ideas that is genuinely unique to them. I would argue that Dreamers are better at using their imagination and thinking about the "what if"s of their products and about what it takes to do the work to complete or execute their creative vision.

A CREATIVE ADULT

As I entered the workforce after graduating from college, I was happy with my job, but I always felt something was missing. I found I had a creative calling that had gone unanswered for too long. To fill this gap, I returned to photography and cooking, both creative pursuits I had loved since childhood.

With so much free time outside of work, I began to seek other creative outlets. I tried everything from photography, to watercoloring, to writing, and even playing the ukulele. None of those creative outlets provided the release I was looking for, so I turned to podcasts and blogs, devouring information on how creative people maintained their creativity and a work-life balance.

I was and remain completely inspired by the Dreamers I interviewed for this book. This group of Dreamers would help to guide me along the way to where I needed to go or what I needed to experience to grow and learn to become a creator.

INTRODUCING THE DREAMERS

The creatives I interviewed represent a variety of fields and different paths to creativity and entrepreneurship. They include watchmakers, photographers, podcasters, a nutrition coach, a bespoke shoemaker, media consultants, an architect and industrial designer, a woodworker, and an antique hunter. These are the Dreamers:

- Tim Bent
  - Tim Bent is the owner and founder of the British specialty shop Bentley's, which focuses on beautiful handmade luggage and Edwardian accessories; Tim's store looks like the office of the most interesting man in the world. Tim has been seeking items with the best craftsmanship since 1980 and has no end in sight. He loves to find the next piece and see what is around the corner.

- Maximilian Büsser
  - Max Büsser is a born creator. He is the epitome of the Ursula K. Le Guin quote, "A creative adult is the child who survived." Max is the founder and creative

director of Maximilian Büsser and Friends (MB&F). He is steadfast in his need to create, and creating for him is an addiction. Max creates not just watches, but watches that are deeply personal to him and represent traditional watchmaking interpreted as 3D mechanical and kinetic art.

- George Glasgow Jr.
  - George Glasgow Jr. is the CEO of George Cleverley, a traditional British bespoke shoemaker. George travels the world to meet with clients and still finds time to design new shoes, develop and source new materials, and maintain a healthy work-life balance. George began his career in banking but slowly found himself working with his dad on the bespoke business, taking time off from work to go to trunk shows with his father. George is an incredibly creative marketer and product developer, understanding the intricacies of what his customers will appreciate.

- Melise Gramm
  - Melise Gramm is the creative force and woodworker behind Root Down Organic Furniture. Melise became very interested in classic woodworking and taught herself Italian to pursue training from master craftsmen in Italy in restoration and conservation of wooden furniture. Now living and working in Colorado, Melise creates from reclaimed and natural found wood and works to develop creative pieces within her core ethos of sustainability.

- Ted Gushue
  - Ted Gushue started his career looking for a job in finance at the height of the recession. Unable to find one, Ted tread his own path working in consulting, DJing, and building digital magazines. From this basis, Ted fused his passion for the automobile (specifically Porsche), photography, and building digital content. Ted now runs ERG Media and consults with Porsche and other brands on their digital strategy. His Instagram is bucket-list-worthy, and he lives the jet set lifestyle every day.

- Steve Hallock
  - Steve is the Founder of TickTocking.com, a website where he educates the public on independent watchmaking and sells a curated selection of independent watches. Steve built a software platform, dabbled in venture, and found himself constantly interested in watches, becoming a moderator of a forum. From there, Steve realized that watches were always filling up his free time and the blank spaces in his day. Steve would go on to found TickTocking, host a YouTube channel and a podcast, and be willing to discuss watches with anyone.

- Bob Isaac
  - Bob Isaac is an industrial designer and architect who has a machine shop in his apartment and manufactures pens and fine instruments for watches.

Bob is one of those creative people who will use the tools at hand to create whatever he can. Teaching himself how to use a metal lathe, Bob realized he could replace his favorite pen with one of his own making. And he did. Selling his products under the name of Baughb Labs, Bob creates what he wants to on his own schedule.

- Dan Killian
  - Dan Killian is the maker and creative force behind Pricetitution, a game designed to help you get to know your friends better and connect on a deeper level with people through the guise of silliness. Dan is one of the most creative people I know. He won investment on *Shark Tank* after deciding to apply forty-eight hours before the open audition. Dan spends time every day creating and has focused diligently on making creativity the core focus of his daily work.

- Erik Anders Lang
  - Erik Anders Lang is the founder of Lang Creative, a creative consultancy focused on the golf industry. Erik is a photographer, documentary filmmaker, and golfer. Erik admits he's not the best filmmaker, or the best golfer, but when he points his camera at golf, he creates amazing content. Erik's creativity is incredibly focused, and his passion for golf and producing beautiful content is unrivaled.

- Sheena Lawrick
  - Sheena is a two-time Canadian Olympian for softball. After finding her way to CrossFit following retirement from the Olympic Team, Sheena taught CrossFit, managed a gym, and helped clients with nutrition. One day she was done. Sheena left her job with no plan but two weeks later had a website, a new business, a co-founder, and was providing clients old and new with customized nutrition plans to help them reach their goals.

- Ming Thein
  - Ming Thein is a Renaissance man but laughs at the suggestion, saying, "I am not from Florence and I cannot grow a beard." He's a former consultant and private equity analyst turned professional photographer, writer, Formula 1 car part designer, and most recently founder of the Ming watch brand. To say he is a busy man is an understatement, but somehow he manages to fit all this in his schedule while maintaining a family life and getting out to race karts or go for a drive to clear his head.

- Kari Voutilainen
  - Kari Voutilainen is a Finnish watchmaker living and working in Geneva. Kari creates beautiful watches inspired by nature, classic cars, and light. Kari has helped launch other brands, and not until two great watchmakers sought him out to tell him he was a fool

for working with others did he believe in himself and build his own workshop.

- Eric Wind
  - Eric Wind is the founder of Wind Vintage, a watch retailer specializing in vintage watches using Eric's expertise writing for online watch site Hodinkee and working for the Christie's auction house. Eric hunts for the most interesting watches in the best condition he can find.

PRINCIPLES OF DREAMING

These Dreamers all have their own route to finding and exploring their creativity. Their first approach to creativity is creating for themselves and then sharing that vision with the world. Most of these Dreamers had a long career path to finding a creative pursuit full time. They all demonstrate that taking a passion and turning it into a business is possible, by looking at the world through a lens of curiosity and creativity.

I set out to understand their journey and to find out if creativity was something that came easily or that took time and attention to develop. In the next section of the book, we will move from learning about regretting and dreaming into practical applications of dreaming. These Principles of Dreaming are what we are going to learn in Chapters 5 through 11. They are the critical lessons that have allowed these Dreamers to be successful in their work and in bringing their vision into the world.

These lessons are distilled from direct interviews with these Dreamers, and I will give specific homework assignments along the way. We will look at each dreamer, learn a bit more about their story, and see how they can help us unlock our own creativity. Creativity is something we are all born with, something we can all claim, and something we need to use and train to keep tapping into it. Whether you feel creative today or not, you can always become more creative.

THE PRINCIPLES OF DREAMING

CHAPTER 5

GET COMFORTABLE BEING UNCOMFORTABLE

―――

AND GIVE YOURSELF PERMISSION TO CREATE

Comfort rarely produces great art.

—MOKOKOMA MOKHONOANA

While I was working in government, I often felt I needed permission to leave and pursue something creative. One day while I was still working in government, I gave myself permission to buy a camera and start shooting photographs again. The entire process was incredibly liberating. Slowly, I started to post these photos on Instagram to put myself out there in the world. I had to give myself permission and talk myself into posting the photographs I had taken. And I started to wonder: did other creatives struggle with the need for permission to pursue their creativity?

As it turns out, curiosity is creativity. In every job I have ever held, no matter how great, I have always found this quiet discomfort within myself that I had more to offer, more to give, and needed to find a creative outlet which would allow that fulfillment. Writing was a start for me; this book is just the start in a thousand-mile journey of my own.

Dan Killian and I spoke about that discomfort, that disquiet in the pit of your stomach asking, then begging and pleading, to be fed. The camera helped me post more of my photographs, take more pictures, and learn about photography. Most importantly, photography provided an outlet for my creativity. It was my gateway drug.

Part of the Dreamer's journey is simply getting started: finding an outlet for your creativity and answering the call. You may set out to pursue one area of creativity, and it may open a whole different world for you.

If you are reading this book, you have likely reached a point of discomfort in feeling disconnected from your creativity. Or a discomfort with your career, knowing that you could be doing more creative work. By getting to a point of discomfort, you can more easily get comfortable with creativity, because you can give yourself permission to create just for yourself. You don't have to start creating for anyone else, just create to satisfy your own curiosities to start. If you wait for the right moment to start, it will never come. If you keep delaying, you will never get yourself out of the place of disquiet and discomfort. We are about to go on a journey to learn how to get comfortable.

GETTING PERMISSION

After spending time at the gym as a coach, Sheena Lawrick became a manager and grew deeply interested in nutrition, having an opportunity to work one-on-one with clients. As those roles shifted, Sheena gravitated toward nutrition coaching and realized she just needed to jump and start a business. But Sheena felt the need for permission, telling herself she wouldn't succeed on her own, practicing convergent thinking, telling herself that any idea of striking out on her own was certain to be met with doom. Recognizing this need, she started thinking about how to grant herself permission to pursue a career path on her own.

Sheena found that working with a therapist helped her recognize this need and grant herself permission to pursue new work. Receiving this permission, Sheena realized she was at the end of the road with her job and had a vacation coming up. With no future plans, Sheena decided that when she left for vacation, she should leave her job to find out what was next.

Fortuitously, one of her former clients was focused on nutrition and wanted to team up on a business. Sheena found that having a business partner made the transition easier and reduced the element of fear of failure. She describes this process as "somebody just handed you this opportunity where you're like, 'this is too good to be true.' . . . So we honestly ran with it." People quickly realized that Beyond the Box Nutrition had opened, and they asked Sheena how long it had taken to get a business plan, a website, pricing, plans, and a client base together. She responded honestly, "Two weeks!"

This perceived requirement or feeling of needing permission to go out and do something on her own is not uncommon for Sheena. And this question comes up repeatedly for creators who want to take their side project or creative project and turn it into a business. You need to know where you are feeling held back and understand what you need to do to change that, and from whom you need permission to proceed. It may be easier to start with the "why?"

Often, self-doubt brings into question the vision we want to see in the world. Getting permission from a spouse, family, a friend to pursue this creative work may be the key to unlocking your creativity. Spend some time thinking about why you need permission to begin in the first place. Is the vision scary? What scares you about it? These are good areas to begin looking at your creativity and interacting with it to give yourself permission to create.

DISCOMFORT

One reason we often don't allocate the resources for our creative projects is that we haven't yet given ourselves permission to create. However, we have to begin in earnest by planning. We simply need to allocate one resource: time. The only thing you likely need to get started is your brain, a willingness to come to the table dreaming with a pen and paper to start writing down ideas and creating as many ideas that might fulfill your creative needs as possible. Only after all ideas are laid out on paper can we actually begin to disqualify ideas that do not set your creativity on fire and get you excited to create.

One aspect that separates Dreamers from Regretters is a willingness to act. It is the *need* to give themselves permission and take action that motivates Dreamers. They need to get to a place where they are so uncomfortable with the lack of creativity or applying creativity in their daily life and work. They realize that attempting to fulfill their creative vision is a far higher priority than the stability associated with staying in their current role. Realizing this limitation, they give themselves permission to go out into the world and bring their vision into being.

After eight and a half years at an advertising firm, Dan Killian quit his job with a very limited plan to pursue the creation of his card game, Pricetitution, full time. In leaving his position, Dan created a sense of uncertainty and discomfort, but it was exactly the comfort level he needed to continue on his creative journey. After completing his game, launching it to the market, and receiving additional funding from ABC's *Shark Tank*, Dan is still amazed at the number of people who come up to him and tell him that he "made it."

Dan's response to former coworkers is that "I haven't made it by any means yet. I still don't know what I'm doing. But this idea of one of us got out . . . it makes you realize that maybe you're not that failure for doing this, you might be the success story . . . so whether you do it one year in, nine years in, or thirty years later and make the change, it feels like that's a win. That's a big win, because lots of people don't take the leap that they want to."

Dan points out something so important to this narrative of getting uncomfortable. While you have to plan and use your time wisely, whether you are uncomfortable in your current job because it lacks creativity or otherwise, you know you are capable of more or just aren't sure you fit in. No matter the case, even working for yourself on your own project is going to be uncomfortable. It is going to come with potential lean time, times of fear, uncertainty, and doubt, so you must prepare yourself for that. But what you cannot do—you absolutely cannot let it hold you back from bringing your vision into the world.

GETTING UNCOMFORTABLE

Melise Gramm is a portrait of getting uncomfortable to learn new skills. She is now the tour de force and creator behind Root Down Organic Furniture, her workshop focused on sourcing reclaimed wood from Southeast Asia. Melise has been interested in classic woodworking for a long time and since decided to make a career of it.

Following a stint working in advertising and realizing that the competitive nature of the business was not what she wanted to pursue over the course of a career, Melise began working for a shop that repaired wood furniture, better known as "scratch, dent, and gouge" work. After learning the company she was working for had declared itself a "restoration shop," she became curious about what this term meant and started researching.

Melise wanted to understand exactly what being a furniture restorer meant, and her research uncovered that very few furniture restorers operated in the United States, or even in the world. She was immediately taken with the idea of getting into this business.

She began to look at graduate study programs, which were located in the United Kingdom and Italy, where she would learn from master craftsmen in furniture repair. "I was going to train in England, and I just thought if I am going to move overseas and learn a new trade, I might as well go all the way. So I taught myself Italian and moved to Italy."

While working at her "scratch, dent, and gouge" job, she would work with her headphones on, listening to Italian lessons. With four months of Italian practice and learning, Melise felt comfortable enough with her Italian to apply.

"When I arrived at the airport, I knew just enough Italian to get me in trouble. I answered my taxi driver back in pretty much perfect Italian, and then he just went off like I would understand what he was saying, and that's when I realized that I didn't really know Italian at all."

Melise was so shy in the first few months in her restoration program that she hardly said a word, but she understood all the conversations happening around her. After that, she opened up and started speaking more.

Getting uncomfortable being comfortable pushed Melise to attend graduate school in Italy, to learn Italian, and to try something radically different. When she came back to the United

States, she returned to Colorado and began working immediately with interior designers and galleries, initially completing restoration work but soon began branching out into her own work.

She now focuses on creations from reclaimed wood through her workshop, Root Down Organic Furniture. This work allows Melise to express her creativity as she lets the structures of the reclaimed wood dictate what she makes from each piece. "It is freeing. It is in that I kind of just get lost. I would say that in those moments of creativity I get lost and where I can just whittle away the hours." Getting uncomfortable and forcing herself to work in a new language allowed Melise to learn a trade that would allow her to fully express her creativity.

GET COMFORTABLE BEING UNCOMFORTABLE

One of the things that truly influenced me was an Instagram post from Ted Gushue that I saw a few days after we spoke. Someone had posed the question to Ted of how to be more like him. Ted asked the follower to absolutely not do this. "Trying to be like me or anyone else will ensure that you are always number two, and I want you to be number one. Be the best that you can be and learn and borrow from everyone and everything that inspires you."[37]

I started thinking about what this meant more broadly, not just for creatives but for all working professionals. Various people, brands, and art have clearly inspired us to pursue a

---

37   Gushue, Ted [@tedgushue]. (2019, July 5). I'm Stuck in a Car for 5 hours. What do you want to know?

craft, but we can see a fine line between differentiating your work from someone else and being inspired by them, while not being like them or copying their work.

This concept really resonated with me. Bring yourself to the party; don't be anyone else—be yourself. In other words, don't put on a front to act like me or anyone else in the room. Be yourself, let your personality show. Showcase the product, but do it in your own way. And one of the things I repeatedly heard from Dreamers was to be yourself and follow your own gut to develop that sense of self, style, or method.

Your personality and skills create a path that only you can follow—you just have to know how to tease those elements out and how to combine them. By bringing yourself to the party, you can begin to understand what drives you and what makes you tick. What elements do you know you are good at in your creative pursuit? Where are you falling short? Developing an intuitive sense of your brand DNA will help identify the target customer and strategy to reach them. Ted Gushue put it well in saying: "Like building any religion, sometimes the followers just come out of the woodwork."

HOMEWORK

Think about what's holding you back from pursuing your creativity or presenting it to the world. Do you need permission from your family to do creative work? Do you need permission from yourself? You have to do a lot of deep work here, so talking this matter through with a friend or journaling about it are helpful to the creative process. Sometimes you just need to get over the initial fear to put something on Instagram, post an article to your blog, or publish your first video on YouTube. I give you permission to get started on the work that is going to help you bring your creative vision into the world. Get some Post-it Notes and start writing down ideas. Grab a sheet of paper and just start writing, set a time for twenty minutes, and go.

I guarantee at the end of the twenty minutes, you will feel like no time has elapsed and feel completely energized to do more. Don't burn yourself out, but work in steady increments to generate ideas. In the next few chapters, we look at how the best and brightest creative minds actually structure their time and create a point to think about what they are working on. This method will provide some ideas, but for now twenty minutes of active divergent thinking, just generating ideas, will help to start the creativity engine and get you in the habit of creating daily.

CHAPTER 6

CURIOSITY OVER FEAR

———

What sets you apart can sometimes feel like a burden and it's not. And a lot of the time, it's what makes you great.

—EMMA STONE

After much contemplation on the subject, I found the biggest difference between Regretters and Dreamers is the way they interpret opportunities. Regretters see the potential downsides to an opportunity, the risk, the change of failure, the negatives in a situation. Dreamers, on the other hand, look at an opportunity and see myriad ways in which they could apply their creativity to it.

Dreamers set themselves apart from others in the way they make decisions to prioritize curiosity over fear. They are often more curious to find out if they can deliver the solution to a problem, or what kind of solution they might develop, rather than worrying about failure. This mix of a belief in themselves and a curious nature is one of the most peculiar and fascinating aspects of Dreamers.

Erik Anders Lang, a Dreamer, may best be known for his work in the golf industry. He is the brains and talent behind the YouTube series "Adventures in Golf," exploring all facets of the world of golf, and the host of the Erik Anders Lang podcast. But working in the golf industry was never the intended plan—it just kind of fell into place.

Erik started in photography, learned the technical aspects from one of the most well-known landscape photographers, and wanted to follow in his footsteps. "I was always interested in photography. I would take these old vintage cameras out into the woods and take photos of trees and landscapes, and Ansel Adams was my hero."

Erik soon found that it wasn't always that easy. Erik wanted to become a photographer but had to pay bills. He spent time working in diners in New York, shooting portraits, and continuing to develop his craft as a portrait photographer.[38] Erik would pose subjects for portraits, deliberately consider lighting, angle, reason for the portrait, and what story he wanted to tell with it. He would then shoot a few frames and the commission would be completed.

Erik's work in portrait photography eventually led to a job as an assistant for David LaChapelle, a well-known commercial and fine art photographer. Working with LaChapelle for

---

38 Erik Anders Lang, "Ep 97: Erik Discusses How he Got Into Making Golf Content, A Round with a New Golfer and How Nothing in Life is Personal," Erik Anders Lang Show, January 21, 2019. Los Angeles, CA, Podcast, 01:01:49.

about two years, Erik was exposed to a style of photography entirely different from his own. He would learn that these shoots would take half an hour; they would shoot tons of frames and be done.

During this time Erik discovered video as a creative medium. "I found video at the suggestion of a couple friends, and basically I was hired to do a portrait of this artists Takashi Murakami and he was like, 'Do you know anybody who could make a documentary for me?' And I said, 'If you give me half the money upfront I will do it.'" Erik had accepted his first video commission, though not without some trepidation.

"It sort of comes down to curiosity over fear. You have to trust on some level that you can accomplish it at least 51 percent. It's okay to be completely afraid, as long as you are a little bit more curious about what it takes to succeed." Erik was more curious to see if he could succeed at creating a documentary than he was afraid to fail. With that attitude, Erik dove in and produced the documentary, and the client was completely satisfied with the production.

Erik laughs as he tells me that when he looks back on that documentary, he thinks it is bad, but it was a gateway to get him started. His curiosity overcame his fear of failure, and he delivered the end product to the client. At the same time, Erik was finding himself deeper and deeper in love with the game of golf.

GET STARTED

The hardest thing to do in any creative endeavor is to get started. You can complain that you do not have the right materials, the right paints, the right word processor, but the simple fact is that you just have to start. Once you start, you gain momentum that will carry you. Getting started is so hard because we are all afraid to put ourselves out there, to be vulnerable. We will learn methods to help set a trap for creativity in Chapter 8.

During my conversation with Sheena, she clarified on this point for me when I asked if she had ever really felt stuck. "I don't know why, but it comes down to a series of choices. And sometimes you just . . . you can talk yourself out of anything, or you can talk yourself into anything. And at the end of the day, it just comes down to one day, you're gonna have to make a choice. Otherwise, you're just wasting time." And I realized that I had just been wasting time, digging my heels in and holding on to my limitations and my limiting beliefs, rather than getting started.

As I look around at other entrepreneurs, I realized if they could do it, so could I. Everyone has felt a bit stuck at some point in their life. The Dreamers in this world figure out how to get started and turn being stuck into a competitive advantage. The key (whether you are just starting a creative journey or know that you have to create on your own) is that no matter what, your unique skills and experiences are what will set you up for success. Steve Hallock put it best: "Your personality carries you, or your particular set of skills will

kind of create some sort of path that then you can either kind
of follow and expand on or a lot of people, I think, just don't
notice it, shut it down."

Don't give up on yourself if you don't know where that path
leads yet. Chase those threads of curiosity and understand
them. That is, then, the place where you can start to build from
to pursue your creativity, or unleash your creativity on the
feeling and dig around what is at the center of it. Chances are,
a path will unfold before you once you choose to get started.

PROTOTYPE ASAP

Speaking with Pricetitution creator Dan Killian, I found
it clear that Dan did not want to wait for a market to catch
up to him. He wanted to build a product, refine it through
testing in the market, and get it out into the hands of end
users as quickly as possible. Dan would work tirelessly at creating ideas for Pricetitution and work to beta-test them with
friends before including them in the game. When he felt he
had enough ideas, Dan headed to a bar in his neighborhood
with many board game options.

Dan would find a group finishing their game and ask them
if they would be interested in beta-testing a new card game.
He would explain the rules and let them play, watching
and taking notes, understanding exactly how each card
landed, whether the game was successful, and whether
people were enjoying themselves. The greatest metric for
success that Dan found was that players stopped playing

the game and began a deeper conversation about why they chose the answers they did.

This ability to rapidly prototype lends itself to actually getting more creative and learning from your creativity. One of the most important things Dreamers do is to prototype their idea and start sharing it with others immediately. They don't hold onto it waiting for the right time, the right moment—they get started. They try, fail, and learn along the way.

BE AUTHENTIC

When I was training salespeople and working in account management, I used to tell people that you had to bring yourself to the party. I would tell this to new salespeople to demonstrate that knowing the pitch and all the materials, being able to answer technical questions, and deeply understanding our product were the qualities we were looking for. But if you wouldn't smile, laugh, and improvise from the demo script, people would never be interested in buying our product. They wanted to see real people who were able to work a demo with questions in real time and respond to those asks. "Bring yourself to the party" was simply a euphemism for show up and be yourself.

Merriam-Webster's dictionary defines authenticity, as I use it in this case, as being "true to one's own personality, spirit, or character." And we all grew up knowing exactly what we liked and didn't like and would easily express that with explosions of joy and glee, running around like a crazy-pants, or by imploding in a temper tantrum, plopping down right in the middle of aisle seven at the grocery story, throwing our heads back, and wailing.

I began to wonder what had changed in all of us from childhood to adulthood that we no longer immediately ran to the things that gave us joy. I would argue that as we attend school, accept social norms, and start to mature, we inherit a set of standard molds for behavior and creativity. Somewhere along the way we forget to live the way humans were meant to. As Dr. George Land points out, we tend to have the creativity taught out of us at some stage or another, and as we grow up, we become less creative. However, understanding your authentic self and voice will help guide you to a creative project.

Understanding where you are coming from, to know what you like and what you don't like, so as to not chase the wrong creative project, is critical. In Chapter 8, you will learn about Essentialism and how we often end up chasing the wrong project or idea. Being authentic will help you identify those ideas that do not resonate with you, and while you can still learn from chasing the wrong idea or creative project, doing so can lead you astray from finding the right project.

I started wondering about authenticity and how creatives moved between clients and projects, helping customers in a corporate voice while maintaining their own perspective and bringing fresh eyes to projects and clients—or, bringing themselves to the party. As I spoke to the creative entrepreneurs featured here, I found that a central theme for their reason to pursue creative work was an authenticity they could not bring to other jobs or in working for other people.

After fourteen years working for other watch brands and revitalizing their product lines, Max Büsser is a Dreamer who had to rediscover his creativity to create something that felt authentic to him. Max admits that he and his father were never close, but the passing of his father had a major impact on him. This event led Max to therapy, working through his father's passing, and during his therapy Max realized he needed to create for himself and could no longer create for other people.[39] Realizing that revitalizing existing watch brands was no longer fulfilling his creative need, Max left and started his own company, Maximilian Büsser and Friends.

Max is a self-admitted geek, who had no friends as a kid,[40] which led him deep into the world of sci-fi and adventure, and that is exactly the knowledge Max called upon when

39 Maximilian Büsser and Stephen Pulvirent, "Hodinkee Radio Episode 26: Maximilian Büsser," Hodinkee Radio Podcast, January 7, 2019, New York City, NY, podcast, 01:08:48.

40 Büsser and Pulvirent, "Hodinkee Radio Episode 26: Maximilian Büsser."

creating the design language for MB&F. Resigning from his job, Max spent two years in his flat creating, sketching and imagining his product line. His product was completely different from what was accepted as traditional watchmaking. Max wanted to take the idea of watchmaking as art and create a 3D mechanical art that also told the time.

Max's first watch was not traditional in any sense of the word, and most retailers and watch industry insiders told him he was crazy. Luckily, six retailers saw the sketch for the first product and decided to buy into the concept. This concept was so personal to Max and so authentic to his core that he needed to bring it to life because no one was out in the world doing what he wanted to.

Max knows that, to be truly free, he has to create, and create on his terms. "I don't care if there is any client who wants to buy it. Create what you really believe, even though your engineers tell you you are insane and it is never going to be possible to do. And just bulldoze ahead and make your dream come true. And when it's true, when it's in your hand and the heart is beating for you, you've created your child, and this is your child. And that moment is over priceless. No marketeer can ever understand that moment. So that is what I do."[41]

Authenticity also shows in creative projects. People know when you are being real and when you are being fake. This idea is exactly where my theory of bringing yourself to the

---

41   Interview with Author, July 8, 2019.

party came from: a point of authenticity. When I found myself in a room full of potential clients, I knew they would see through any veneer I put up. I decided being myself and just working from a place of authenticity was far better, that they would make a better choice based on whether they liked me and what I had to say.

BACK TO ERIK

Erik's brother repeatedly asked him if he wanted to play golf, and Erik always turned him down. He simply believed he was not a golfer, but really had no idea what he was saying "no" to. As luck would have it, his brother kept asking, and Erik finally relented. And he fell in love with the game of golf.

Erik quickly realized that he wanted to keep playing golf and get deeply involved in a creative project involving golf. Erik decided that an interesting approach would be to point his camera at golf and see what came out from the camera. "I was continuing the film and had formed an idea for a movie, which at the time was going to be called 'Golf the Hole Story.' I've since changed the name to 'Be the Ball,' but that is the makings of a film that is yet to come out that's still very much in progress, about the mental side of golf, finding that there was this subset of a subset of golfers that use meditation to advance their golf game, whether it was amateurs or number one in the world Jason Day, who's obviously in the film as a subject, and we staged an experiment."

As Erik began working on the documentary, his friends pushed him to cut his own fundraising trailer, which wasn't something he was entirely comfortable with. "I thought I had to pretend to be a golfer. And so I made this trailer where I was like, 'Hi I'm Erik, I'm gonna make a golf movie.' And, you know, my friends were like, 'Why don't you just be yourself and be funny, and you wear a t-shirt and play golf course and municipal golf course and just be yourself?' Well, I am a little more curious than I am afraid of failing, so I tried it, and it was really funny and, like, we're cracking each other up in the editing room and I was like, 'This is funny.'"

And that trailer would garner some more interesting attention. "The real lightning moment was when the PGA Tour saw these clips and said, 'Geez, you'd make a good host.'" Erik toyed with this idea for a moment and turned down the offer. Erik was convinced that his only skill was behind the camera and in the editing room as a documentary filmmaker. But they were insistent and Erik, being more curious than afraid to fail, tried it. And it worked. And that series of edits became season one of "Adventures in Golf." "That was me dipping my toe into actually being an on-camera personality."

Erik's story is unique. He had a skillset and opportunities, but by diving deeply into golf and then continuing to follow a dream, Erik was able to build his own creative business around golf. Now his company, Lang Creative, focuses solely on golf, which keeps him busy. Erik has had offers to work on other projects, to branch out to other sports, but he can't bring himself to do it. He still thinks he has so much work to do with golf.

HOMEWORK

What amazes me about Dreamers is that each of them had a moment when they had to choose curiosity over fear, when they knew they needed to pursue something, whether watchmaking, working on their own, nutrition coaching, or building digital strategies for multinational corporations. They all found the intuition within themselves to understand what they needed to do next and how to find the path to get there.

So what makes you different? Look at your past experiences and understand what is unique about them. Then write that list down and start thinking about how those things turn into strengths, apply the Dreamer framework of divergent thinking, and start connecting dots to your work and life experiences and your personality. This approach provides a framework for turning perceived weakness into strength, and perceived differences into strategic key differentiators that make your business unique and ensure that you are the only person suited to actually building and running this business.

CHAPTER 7

TIME AND DREAMS

The only way to do great work is to love what you do. If you haven't found it yet, keep looking. Don't settle.

—STEVE JOBS

When I look at a creative project, I get very excited. I start off with mounds of motivation and I begin writing a big-picture strategy and developing a big-picture vision of all the ideas. And as I move away from the big picture to the tactical nitty-gritty details, I find myself losing interest. My motivation wanes as I realize the enormity of the task in front of me, and that motivation often turns to trepidation.

To begin a creative journey, you must first recognize the hurdles standing in your way. Looking at a creative project and knowing how to take it forward often feels quite difficult. Sometimes the end goal, the dream, seems so big and looms so large that it feels incredibly difficult to execute on it. I certainly find myself overwhelmed by trying to take that first step.

On Bond Street's "The Nitty Gritty Podcast" on July 25, 2017, Ellen Bennett, founder of Hedley & Bennett, recounts stories of cooking and managing household finances to support her mom. Ellen explains that when she was a child, she wanted to help her mother and make her mom's life easier.[42] Early in life, Ellen learned how to break down problems into manageable pieces.

One way Ellen could accomplish this task was to cook for her mother. She realized that to do so she would need to buy groceries. To go to a grocery store, she needed money and transportation there and back. "I just broke it down into tangible actions and executed on it. And business, however complicated it may seem, is comprised of a ton of little actions. And if you break them down and do them one by one, or sometimes ten by one, or twenty at the same time, you can get to the grocery store, so to speak."[43]

Ellen was able to help support her mom by recognizing the scale of the challenge in front of her and then breaking that challenge down into smaller and smaller pieces. Perhaps the biggest hurdle on the way to achieving your creative goals is understanding what you need to be working on and how to find the time. As this chapter will show, you can find ways and means of overcoming these potential roadblocks. We just like to make things more complicated.

The thirty-two different business ideas I have are pulling me in too many different directions. Each idea has so

---

42 Ellen Bennett and David Haber, "The Nitty-Gritty Podcast: Hedley & Bennett," Podcast, July 25, 2017, New York City, NY, Podcast, 1:04:17.

43 Bennett and Haber, "The Nitty-Gritty Podcast: Hedley & Bennett," 5:36.

many little component pieces. I never quite know what I am going to wake up to and feel like working on any given day. This uncertainty has left me feeling the fear of missing out on a project and like I needed to turn every hobby I have into a business idea. While a lot of my business ideas have come from hobbies, I know now I must create a defined, clear path and build structure in my daily schedule to pursue creativity and move toward my own creative goals. I need to choose an idea and move forward with it, one piece at a time.

ESSENTIALISM

I have often fallen down the rabbit hole of what Greg McKeown, author of *Essentialism: The Disciplined Pursuit of Less*, referred to as stormtroopers in his interview on Tim Ferriss' podcast. Stormtroopers come into your life looming large and seeming important to achieve or attain, and as soon as you arrive or get to the cusp of achievement, you wonder why the hell you wasted your time chasing it in the first place.[44] He instead argues that we should learn to let go of the things, ideas, and beliefs that are no longer serving us. When I heard that metaphor, I realized I had, and still do, chase many stormtrooper ideas and beliefs. And perhaps the time had come to start figuring out what in my world was essential to me, what was no longer serving me, and what I was willing to let go of to pursue my creativity.

---

44   Greg McKeown and Tim Ferriss, "Greg McKeown – How to Master Essentialism (#355)," *The Tim Ferriss Show*, January 9, 2019, San Francisco, CA, podcast, 01:37:31.

McKeown is a big proponent of designing your life around what is essential to you, eliminating all the beliefs, actions, and daily requirements that are nonessential to you, and building structure to achieve those essential tasks with as little effort as possible. He describes the process of finding out what is essential to your work by thinking of something you are underinvesting in. For me, I know that something is creating a business and putting all my effort into trying to actually launch a creative pursuit. McKeown then asks you to identify the "why" behind this idea, why it matters to you, to define what amount of daily time you need to invest to feel as though you are making a meaningful contribution to it.[45]

With this information, you can begin planning what you need to do to commit to this project and know exactly what it looks like to succeed. McKeown also points out that you have to be careful with what you tell yourself about this project and be sure to be aware of your emotional response—are you afraid someone will judge you for it? Are you scared to put yourself out there on social media? Are you afraid of failing? Take note of those emotions and change the narrative in your head to say that people may judge, but you recognize the importance of the work for yourself. Much of creativity is dictated by what you personally deem important, so you should pursue that work because it will likely resonate with others.

Cal Newport, author of *Deep Work*, is a computer science professor at Georgetown University and focuses his research

---

45 McKeown and Ferriss, "Greg McKeown – How to Master Essentialism (#355)."

on how to use digital tools more effectively to do the work we care about and be less distracted by the emerging technologies around us. He is a proponent of "deep work," or what he refers to as "the ability to concentrate without distraction on a demanding task."[46] He argues that deep work is becoming increasingly harder with the rise in technology and is an increasingly rare skill.

Newport suggests that people end up loving their work because they develop a craftsman mindset, working on solving hard challenges that are meaningful to them while getting better at their job over time, and not because they were following their passion. He argues that working hard is actually what will make you happy. He also argues that by finding ways to do deep work and cultivate your ability to concentrate intensely without distraction, you are able to achieve more and generate higher levels of concentration, and I would argue creativity, by generating more flow of thinking in your daily life.[47] To do so, you have to limit your distractions and actually block off the time to think and create.

Dan Killian sums up this necessity well. According to Dan, you "have to define the finish line before you start, which I don't think that you need to do that when you're general

---

46 Cal Newport, "About Me," Cal Newport, accessed September 2019.
47 Cal Newport, "Cal Newport – Deep Work, Digital Minimalism, and the Key to a Happy Retirement," Financial Independence Podcast, March 5, 2019, podcast, 49:16, https://podcasts.apple.com/us/podcast/cal-newport-deep-work-digital-minimalism-key-to-happy/id540593710?i=1000431124693

brainstorming . . . but knowing what success is for you, or the end goal, I think that's super important. How you get there isn't important, but you have to know what the end goal is, and that doesn't mean you are going to end up there." Define your goal and start your journey; you have no guarantee that you will get where you intend to go, yet you may end up somewhere better than imagined.

REMOVING DISTRACTION

Finnish watchmaker Kari Voutilainen removes all distractions and only focuses on the task in front of him. As a result of his mandatory military service, Kari attributes a lot of his work habits to having a singularly focused mind. "Very often when I am at home and I work, I am very focused to do what I am doing, so I don't have time. I am concentrating on what I am doing. And like a military mind, I really plan my day." Without knowing it, Kari is a proponent of the Cal Newport "deep work" philosophy: when he arrives at work, he tunes out all external distractions and works only on the project at hand.

Kari is not distracted by the hype of sales and marketing; he doesn't even employ a sales team. He goes to two watch shows a year, one in New York and one in Basel, Switzerland. The rest of the time, Kari is deeply focused on creating. Even Kari's downtime—shooting photography, hiking, skiing—is dedicated to learning more about and honing his craft. These experiences influence him, his style choices, how he makes each watch.

John Thompson, global head of advanced analytics and artificial intelligence at CSL Behring, is a published author working on his second book. When I asked him about his writing process, he replied that he wakes up early, somewhere between 3 and 5 a.m., and writes for about one to three hours each morning. John's secret to his productivity, aside from waking up early, is that he has been a proponent of turning off the WiFi when he goes to bed. "That fact alone has increased my writing productivity. I write until I am done for the day and then go turn the WiFi on and engage in social media, check email, and all the normal online activities. I find that writing consistently in the morning makes me feel like I do when I have just left the gym, relaxed and happy."[48]

John's argument is that, to write a book, he simply needs to sit down and write, distraction-free. He admits that setting a goal simply to write daily is a low bar, "but to do it consistently with something to say makes the whole effort truly enjoyable."[49] Find a creative pursuit and create time to do it every day. Then it becomes something that you are not forcing yourself to do, but something you are choosing to spend your time doing above other activities, giving it value and, hopefully, like John, leaving you "relaxed and happy."[50]

48 Thompson, John [John Thompson]. December, 2019. Response to LinkedIn Post regarding John's new book and his writing process.
49 Thompson. December, 2019. Response to LinkedIn Post regarding John's new book and his writing process.
50 Thompson. December, 2019. Response to LinkedIn Post regarding John's new book and his writing process.

BLOCK TIME TO WORK

With twenty-four hours in a day, you have to understand how you spend those hours and where you can unlock time to create. To start dreaming, we need some structure and framework, and from there, we can understand our vision and creative goals, structure around them, and execute against a plan to make that creative vision come to life.

This point is where one of the most important lessons from the Dreamers interviewed in this book comes in: you absolutely have to look at how your time is spent every day and understand what takes up your free time, or the blank space within your day.

The first step is looking at how you are spending time in a given day. Do you rise early or sleep in? Perhaps you can be like John Thompson and be creative early in your day; perhaps you are more creative late at night. Understanding how you prefer to structure your routine, and the macro-trends associated with those preferences, will help you begin to plan your day.

Inventorying the time for your responsibilities and creating a daily schedule allows you to see what time is available for you to create. If your creative time is spent on the couch with Netflix on in the background, you are not giving your undivided attention to creativity. Take a look at what you're doing before you go to work and when you come home. Are you watching TV, cooking, caring for your family, working out, or finishing work from earlier in the day?

Looking at this schedule will let you understand what is actually taking up your time and where you might have downtime to pursue creativity. Making an inventory of a week will help you realize the gaps in your schedule and point you directly to the time you can block off to work on a creative project. This time could take the form of going out and shooting photographs on a weekend because that's when you have a free moment, and finding half an hour on a weeknight to edit those photos from the weekend and post them to relevant social media sites to share your creativity.

This concept links back to the Cal Newport theory of having a rigid structure to your day. Many would argue that structure is the antithesis of creativity, but I tend to agree with Newport: structure is freedom, and by planning out your day, you are actually able to work harder on problems that matter to you and to concentrate better for a more structured period of time on the creative vision you want to bring into the world. By planning and creating space for creativity, you are beginning to set the trap for creativity, dreaming, and creating the life you want to see.

LOOKING AT THE BLANK SPACE

Steve Hallock is a great application of this philosophy. Steve experienced success early in life in venture capital and technology, building a technical high-frequency trading platform.[51] This success provided Steve with a sense of accomplishment, hard work, and achievement. Following a move to Los Angeles,

---

51   Hallock, Stephen [Steve Hallock]. December, 2019. LinkedIn Profile.

he became interested in watches. Researching the watch world deeply on all the internet watch forums, Steve not only looked for his first watch, but also built a passion along the way.

Steve quickly started contributing to online watch forums, posting frequently, until he found himself in a position as a moderator on the Purists forum, one of the first major havens for watch-collectors on the internet. From this position, Steve started to meet collectors from all over the world and soon became a conduit for collectors looking to trade or sell watches. Taking a look around at his world, he realized that "watches at some point became the thing that I was doing in between other things, or, you know, had one tab open up something that was always reading and looking at." Realizing that he had the connections and the deal-making, he looked at how he was spending his time.

Curious to explore his new passion, Steve found himself working with Max Büsser of MB&F to launch MB&F North America, building the retail network for the brand across North America, where he built on his network, developed more skills, and learned the business side of the watch industry.

Following his time at MB&F, Steve decided to turn his blog, TickTocking, into a full-time business "helping collectors learn about, find, and buy the good stuff."[52] In our interview, he admits that he never actively tried to enter the watch industry. One day, Steve looked around and realized that watches "keep following me. This keeps being a thing. Maybe

---

52   Steve Hallock, "About Me," TickTocking, accessed August 2019.

I'll just do it. And I can always quit." By looking at what he was spending his time doing, Steve realized the opportunity was right in front of him. He admits that his business has been really successful and really fun because he gets to collect and see interesting watches, meet interesting collectors, and really dive into work that he never really knew about or meant to be a part of.

His attraction to the watch world isn't without some feelings of hesitation, as Steve tells me. "I'm just selling watches, and it seems like a waste of my sort of talent, or whatever. And then on the flip side, I look at it and it's like, well, everybody just sort of does something. And at the end of the day, I don't know that . . . there really are those value judgments beyond just being actually competent and good at what you're doing and creating value somewhere for someone is actually important. It's worked out to be a really good thing, whether I thought they would be or not."

Steve is the perfect example of looking at what is taking up the time around you and following that thread or interest to the fullest possible expression. And one of the most important lessons is that an interest may simply be a stormtrooper you are chasing, but you begin to realize that and you can avoid that trap in the future. Armed with that knowledge, you can change how you filter or pursue creative work in the future. You do really need to identify where and how to focus on finding those things that bring you joy and make you feel creative, and on identifying how much time you need to allocate to those things to feel fulfilled.

HOMEWORK

I do not believe that anyone can *think* their way to a solution for needing more creative outlets in their life. The only way to know with certainty if something gives you creativity and fulfills you is to actually do the work. You actually have to try things and be willing to forego others. Looking at the blank space in your day and what you are doing with your time serves as a good basis for this. You simply have to identify the time of day when you can work on a creative project and block off the time on your calendar.

So the challenge here is to actually catalog what it means to live a creative life for you and identify how you want to use your creativity in your daily life. And I recommend doing this in two phases:

1. Cataloging your daily time; and
2. Writing your dream essay.

Cataloging your daily time is exactly what it sounds like. For a week, track exactly how you are using your time. You can plot out your entire week in the calendar app on your phone or computer or on paper. Are you actually following that exact schedule? Notice if you feel bored such that you immediately flick open your phone to Instagram (guilty), or if when you get home from work you immediately put on Netflix. Become aware of your daily habits and the emotions associated with those habits.

With a better understanding of how our time is spent, we can actually begin to look at how we would ideally spend our time, and structure time in our days to create. This step is the start of building the structure for dreaming.

The perfect plan to become a Dreamer is by writing a dream essay. The goal of this exercise is simple: write out an ideal plan for your life. What kind of work are you doing? What kind of relationship are you in? With whom? Where do you live? Who lives in your house? What kind of house do you own? Do you own a car? What kind of car do you drive? What is your office or studio space like, and who do you work with?

The goal of the dream essay is to map out your dream life. As Dan Killian said, you have to understand the end goal and work backward. So write down the end goal. What fills your days? What kind of work do you do? What is your job title? Where are you living? Where are you working? Getting into painstaking detail will make the dream all the more vivid and allow you to create small goals and objectives to achieve it. You can outline, sketch, create a mind map—but you must dream big.

The importance of dreaming big here is that it kickstarts our creativity, allowing us to open a pathway to divergent thinking. I would advise that writing this essay by hand on paper is a far more effective way to begin. It allows the tactility of writing to start planting the seeds of these dreams in our heads. And when those seeds are planted, we start to dream and think even bigger, identifying our end goal.

With this document as a roadmap, as Ellen Bennet teaches us, we can break our dream down into its component pieces and start actually making decisions and taking action to put into place tangible pieces of our dream to align real life and our dream. This step is the beginning of the thousand-mile journey with creativity.

With the essay completed, take some time to think it over. Does it have all the pieces you want? Does it include all the forms of creativity you want to use on a daily basis? If so, good; if not, revise it. Take as much time as you need to do that. In fact, taking time to think and setting a trap for creativity is one of the key lessons learned from the Dreamers in this book, and we are going to look at in Chapter 8.

SET A TRAP FOR CREATIVITY

———

So take the time to think. Discover your real reason for being here and then have the courage to act on it.

—ROBIN SHARMA

One of the core principles of dreaming is to set a trap for creativity. As we learned in Chapter 7, blocking off time to create allows Dreamers to use that time to accomplish a number of different goals, from ideating a new project concept to finding the appropriate way to close out an existing project. Setting the trap is a daily repetitive action you use to set the scene and invite creativity into your life. The routine of taking this step is important because it compounds over time, helping you become more creative and sink into your creativity faster.

Placing the trap for creativity sets the stage for engaging in creative work. Some days when setting the trap brings creativity, it shows up immediately: words flow onto your page, chords are effortless, the drawings come easily. Other days it doesn't quite work like that. However, showing up and using the same method or combination of methods every day to invite creativity into your life establishes a routine that will signal your brain to switch modes and enter a more creative state.

Most of the Dreamers I spoke to manage complex businesses, have families, and must accomplish myriad tasks every day. Through this lens, I started asking creatives how they blocked off the time and how they set a trap for creativity to show up daily in their lives. The most common responses were that creatives took time to themselves to think alone: some worked out or had some form of movement practice, others practiced meditation and breath work, one in particular drove racecars to think, and some chose to write to set a trap for creativity.

In this chapter, we will explore different methods that Dreamers use to trap creativity, allowing them to discover inspiration daily, find a flow state, and get into their creative work so they may uncover the fullest expression of their ideas.

THINK

Asking Max Büsser how he set a trap for creativity every day, for me, is like getting to ask Leonardo da Vinci how he accomplished so much in his time. When Max began on his solo creative journey to start Maximilian Büsser & Friends, he spent months with friend and designer Eric Giroud to develop his design and create the sketch of his first ever watch. The pair spent months going back and forth looking at the deepest, most creative parts of Max's personality to design the brand language.

Max admits that today he works 100 percent alone. During the ideation and creation phase of a new product, he focuses on his own creativity, listening to the creative voice inside his head for ideas. Max knew that taking time to think was one method that helped him find creative ideas and solidify them into his product and long-term vision for the brand.

How does he accomplish this? Max has designed spaces around his house he calls "creative lounges" that allow him the space he needs to think. Whether he is at home in a creative lounge, on a plane, in a car, or in his garden at home, Max's preferred method to set a trap for creativity is to take an hour, alone, with no phone, no notepad, no devices at all, and just sit and think. "I take an hour every couple of days all alone in the garden (with no phone anywhere close) and allow myself to think. An hour is a very long time of thinking. . . . It is by far my most efficient technique today."[53]

An hour sitting alone is a very long time to think, but I understand where Max is going. Walking away from technology and devices can sometimes unlock an area of my brain required to entertain myself and allow my mind to wander into far recesses that haven't been accessed for years. This stillness,

---

53 Maximilian Büsser, email to the author, July 28, 2019.

lack of devices for immediate gratification, and the necessity of entertaining your brain can allow new ideas to come to light. An hour might be too long to start with, but a fifteen- to twenty-minute session might work.

The idea of the creative lounge is also an interesting concept. Think about where you create best—sitting on the sofa, at the kitchen table, at your local coffee shop? I would let that observation influence setting up your own creative lounge. If you have the space available to make a creative lounge for yourself, you should use it only for your creative work. If you don't, think about the kind of space that does stimulate your creativity and go out looking for that space; try everything until you find somewhere that helps you set a trap for creativity. You may find that the simple process of going for a walk or a ride looking for a space helps to set the trap.

MOVE

In a complete juxtaposition to sitting and thinking, many Dreamers find that movement is the spark that sets the trap for creativity. Sheena Lawrick finds that anything movement-related helps her to "work through stuff." She takes most of her meetings while walking, which helps to stimulate her creativity, despite the background noise of city traffic, construction, or the train. The sights and sounds of the city and the sheer act of moving help her produce new ideas and approaches for working with clients. She believes that movement allows her to create space for clarity, and given her athletic and Olympic background, walking and moving allow her to use her body as an expression of herself she is totally comfortable with, to allow her brain to focus on generating new ideas.

The idea of creating space for new ideas was curious to me. A Stanford study by Marily Oppezzo and Daniel L. Schwartz found that "walking encourages creativity. In three of the alternate uses studies the numbers were profound: 81 percent, 88 percent, and 100 percent of participants were more creative walking than sitting, including on the treadmill."[54] What's interesting is that they used the same test as the open-monitoring meditation study, Guilford's alternate use test.[55]

For me, movement and exercise have always helped set a trap for creativity. Working out unlocks an area of my brain that allows me to problem-solve and create new solutions to the challenges of daily life. While exercising, I routinely generate new ideas, occasionally having to get out a pen and paper and start writing.

A workout first thing in the morning sets up my day for success; it leaves me focused, energized, and helps me to attain a flow state for creative work more easily. While this tactic works for me, I realized that other habits were out there for creatives and I wanted to understand what other creative Dreamers did to stimulate their creativity and work.

---

54 Marily Oppezzo and Daniel L. Schwartz, "Give Your Ideas Some Legs: The Positive Effect of Walking on Creative Thinking.," *Journal of Experimental Psychology: Learning, Memory, and Cognition* 40, no. 4 (2014): pp. 1142-1152.

55 Derek Beres, "How Does the Brain-Body Connection Affect Creativity?," Big Think (Big Think, January 30, 2019).

BREATHE

With all the current discussions around mindfulness practices and morning routines, I know a number of people who swear by meditation and say it absolutely helps them calm down, focus, and unlock their creativity. Erik Lang is even working on a documentary about meditation and golf, linking the two concepts and exploring how some of the world's best golfers use meditation as an on-course tool to help them stay focused.

A study of meditation methods conducted by Lorenza S. Colzato, Ayca Ozturk, and Bernhard Hommel examined focused-attention and open-monitoring forms of meditation. Their work suggests that open-monitoring meditation, a form of meditation in which participants are encouraged to simply see their thoughts, emotions, and sensations yet pass no judgment over them, is the most effective form of meditation.[56]

Simply acknowledging thoughts, emotions, and sensations as they enter your mind, not judging them, and letting them pass, the data suggests, allows for a greater acceptance of our daily range of emotions. This acceptance helps us to better manage the daily stressors within our lives and maintain a more even base every day. This form of meditation, as Colzato and his group found in their study, has a tremendous impact

---

56 Lorenza S Colzato, Ayca Ozturk, and Bernhard Hommel, "Meditate to Create: The Impact of Focused-Attention and Open-Monitoring Training on Convergent and Divergent Thinking," Frontiers in Psychology (Leiden University, Leiden, Netherlands, March 30, 2012).

on creativity. All the test subjects excelled at the divergent thinking required to ideate and generate new ideas after practicing open-monitoring meditation.[57]

One form of meditative practice that shows significant promise for boosting creativity is Wim Hof breathing, a form of deep breath work followed by breath holds that helps reset the body's neurological system. Wim Hof explains the way your breath actually impacts the physiological and chemical reactions that occur within your body.[58] By practicing the Wim Hof method of breathing, you alter the ratio of oxygen and carbon dioxide in the blood, allowing for the body to shift into a more active state.[59] Writer Benjamin McEvoy uses the Wim Hof breathing method and cold exposure to help him trap creativity. As revealed in a July 23, 2016, piece on how writers can improve their writing using the Wim Hof method, Ben found that applying the Wim Hof method helped him increase his daily word output from 1,000 or 2,000 words to 10,000 words per day.[60]

Meditation and the Wim Hof method show tremendous promise for trapping creativity. They open your mind and calm the energy flowing away from you, allowing you to be

57 Colzato et al., "Meditate to Create: The Impact of Focused-Attention and Open-Monitoring Training on Convergent and Divergent Thinking."
58 Isabelle Hof, "The Wim Hof Method Explained," trans. Claire van den Bergh, Wim Hof Method (Enahm Hof / Innerfire, June 2015).
59 Hof, "The Wim Hof Method Explained," trans. Claire van den Bergh.
60 Benjamin McEvoy, "How Writers Can Improve Their Writing With The Wim Hof Method (Review)," Benjamin McEvoy, August 9, 2018.

receptive to creative ideas and energy flowing toward you. These methods are incredibly easy to employ in daily life and require little time to get started. With a number of meditation apps available for smart phones and the praise of greatly increased daily word counts, we can understand why creatives use breathing and mediation to set a trap for creativity.

DRIVE

One of the most interesting methods I found in asking creatives how they set a trap for creativity was by going for a drive. Ming Thein, founder and photographer behind Mingthein. com and the founder of MING Watches, doesn't take time to think without devices or distractions. He sighs and laughs when I ask him what he does to set a trap for creativity. He advises me that with a young family, making a commitment to take time simply to think is difficult. Rather, you can tell that Ming's brain is always ticking; he is always thinking about his business or executing a new business idea.

During our interview, Ming admits that the time he finds most fulfilling is when he is driving, especially manual cars tuned for racing where he really has to focus on driving. He also enjoys relaxation and feels most himself while go-karting, a time when he can really think.[61] This is the type of time that helps Ming write an article or create content, the type of content that can be developed quickly. Ming, however, feels that deeply creative work requires time.

---

61 Ming Thein, in-person meeting with the author, September 3, 2019.

He suggests that his brain likes to think things over for perhaps two months at a time. With that time to think, Ming finds iterating on a product line or developing an entirely new design to be easy, almost as if it happened overnight. Ming believes that deep creativity takes its toll, and this type of deep creativity is not sustainable. He can create deeply to iterate on product and design ideas but in limited sprints, such as two months to revamp a product. He also finds the idea of perpetual, repeated daily creativity to be unsustainable. Once this creative endeavor is complete, he needs time to recover.

Ming's method of setting a trap for creativity is an interesting combination of moving and meditating. By driving, Ming is moving, having to focus on the track, his shifting, managing the car, and other drivers on track. This activity also allows for his conscious mind to focus on the task at hand, while his subconscious brain focuses on the work of creating the design language for Ming Watches, allowing him to really free his brain to fixate on creating while he focuses on winning races. Giving his brain a break to focus on racing allows for his divergent pathways to open up and connect ideas in novel ways.

WRITE

Dan Killian takes a completely separate approach to setting a trap for creativity. Dan found that he actually needed to schedule time for himself to sit down, lock in, and laser-focus on generating ideas. Dan schedules time on his calendar every week, usually for two hours at a time, to sit and think in this practice. "I usually have a Google Doc open and I'm just typing as many bullet points. And I'm organizing them as minimally as possible, because it's more just like putting stuff out there."

This is not an everyday practice for Dan. Sitting and generating ideas for hours can be exhausting, but he finds it incredibly important to keep up the frequency of this practice. He finds that two hours is a minimum of thinking and ideating time, because as he nears the end of his session, enough ideas have been generated that he is able to combine them in novel ways and really start creating something new. And his best ideas come at the end of the session.

By creating many ideas and blocking off time on your calendar to do so, you are asking your brain to enter divergent thinking mode, to actually generate new ideas for yourself. Tracking them in a Google Doc provides you with a digital catalog of ideas, and then, as Dan suggests, near the end of your session your brain can think through ideas from previous sessions and the current session and find new ways to connect them. And once this list has been created, you can judge and rank ideas and actually start developing an idea and strategy that feel like a good match with the vision you want to bring into the world.

CONNECT WITH THE CUSTOMER
George Glasgow Jr. is the CEO of George Cleverley, a classic London-based British bespoke shoemaker. George was brought up in the business, working on weekends and breaks

from school in the workshop, cleaning up, making tea, and packing shoes. He learned from an early age about the world of bespoke and craftsmanship. "I like the idea that, I don't want to say grow old with it, but that you can create stories with it and remember where you ordered. The longer you have it, the more proud you become of it. As clothes, or shoes, or anything ages, I find that so interesting."

Having worked in the bespoke world in some way, shape, or fashion since childhood, George has a keen eye for detail. Often he sets a trap for creativity by traveling to tanneries and understanding their methods of production. He can envision a new product and understand exactly to whom he wants to sell it based on what he knows his customers like.

Often, George draws inspiration from his own customers. They will call, email, or meet with George in person to discuss their unique projects and requests. One customer wanted a pair of shoes that imitated the styling and stitching of the seats in his Ferrari. George and his team studied the photos and the leather and found a way to make it happen. His customers are the best pool of ideas for George, and often they find something quite cool or clever that he can work into the new season or the next trunk show.

George knows something critical and fundamental to his business: connection to the customer. George sets a trap for creativity by connecting with his customers via Instagram, global trunk shows, or having customers stop in at the shop. He is routinely connecting with his customer base and checking in with what samples, what ideas, and what shoes are resonating with them to get a pulse from his core market and understand what he should change, what should be produced, and what core items should remain the same.

TRAVEL

Ted Gushue, founder of ERG Media, who assists Porsche with all of the digital platforms and the *Type 7* magazine, laughs at the question of where he finds inspiration. Ted simply retorts that the only path to inspiration is to "just keep looking at awesome shit all the time." While the suggestion may seem ridiculous, Ted is actually completely right. Not only do you need to keep finding things that inspire you, but you must understand *what* it is that inspires you and how that can inspire you when trying to find a routine in which to set a trap for creativity.

Ted admits that he finds inspiration in design, engineering, art, architecture, and undoubtedly all things Porsche. He admits that "anything that's beautiful and interesting and has a cool story, it kind of draws me in." However, he has found that traveling with other people actually allows him to reinforce his sense of self, helps him understand what he likes, and allows him to set a trap for creativity by seeing something through fresh eyes and getting to explain why something is important to him. Ted also often reflects on the things from which he draws inspiration. He has found that simple mechanical design, engineering, art, and architecture have just drawn him in. He admits that there isn't much else to it: in his interview with Hodinkee Radio, he admitted, "I don't need much. I like the things that I like."[62]

Travel is one of the most fantastic ways to set a trap for creativity. One can never be sure what may occur while traveling, but learning something new and getting to share old favorite places with someone new are always interesting. Travel, as Ted points out, helps to redefine your design aesthetic and may provide inspiration for new work. I have found that flights are a tremendous time to focus on getting work done without anyone bothering me, and often travel time is a great point to set a trap for creativity because you know you are a captive audience for the duration of your flight.

NATURE

One of the best ways I have always found to set a trap for creativity is by spending time in nature. That time allows me relieve some of my stress and allow for downregulation of my neurological system after the weekly overstimulation of cities, traffic, and offices. Simply seeing the colors, feeling the wind and sun on my face, and hearing the myriad sounds in nature allow my brain to turn off all interaction with the modern world. My mind and body immediately feel at peace. The simple act of going for a walk in a forest can immediately change my outlook and put me in a more creative state.

---

62 Ted Gushue and Stephen Pulvirent, "Hodinkee Radio Episode 15: Ted Gushue," Hodinkee Radio Podcast, October 15, 2018, New York City, NY, podcast, 01:07:44.

This effect has been confirmed by numerous studies regarding the psychological benefit of exercising and spending time in nature. A 2011 study from Peninsula College of Medicine and Dentistry found "that most trials showed an improvement in mental well-being: compared with exercising indoors, exercising in natural environments was associated with greater feelings of revitalisation, increased energy, and positive engagement, together with decreases in tension, confusion, anger, and depression. Participants also reported greater enjoyment and satisfaction with outdoor activity and stated that they were more likely to repeat the activity at a later date."[63]

I have always found that time outside in nature leaves me revitalized, calm, and positive, setting an ideal trap for creativity for myself. That calmness allows me to be open to ideas that flow into my brain and permit me the space to explore them. When I return home, I find I can sit down and be incredibly productive, often in a shorter time than would be required had I not spent any time in nature.

LOOK FOR PROBLEMS THAT NEED SOLUTIONS

Bob Isaac is an architect and industrial designer and has been designing things for as long as he can remember. Working on the industrial design team that created the Walkman at

63 J. Thompson Coon et al., "Does Participating in Physical Activity in Outdoor Natural Environments Have a Greater Effect on Physical and Mental Wellbeing than Physical Activity Indoors? A Systematic Review," *Environmental Science & Technology* 45, no. 5 (February 3, 2011): pp. 1761-1772.

Sony really informed Bob's sense of building, developing, and designing products.

Bob is continuously looking for problems to solve with design projects outside of work. "I've always designed products. Initially I just had a need. I would design something." In the early phases of his side project, Baughb Labs, he found that using subcontracted labor for the generation of parts was not only costly but also never fulfilling to Bob. He really wanted to be in the process and not just assembling a final product, but designing, prototyping, and building from scratch the entire time. Bob wanted to make as much as he could in-house. Bob sets a trap for creativity by looking for problems that need solutions.

One day, while inserting a pen refill into his favorite pen, it dawned on Bob that he could build his own. He admits that he never had a plan to sell or market these pens; they was something he just wanted to make for himself. He sat down and started sketching out his ideal pen. That sketch then developed into a 3D model, and before long he was at his lathe shaving down some metal to make a pen. Bob made a run of twenty pens and shared photos on Instagram. His pens sold out immediately.

Bob admits, "There's no way I'm going to get rich. There's no way to make a living. I do it because I love it." But Bob finds his inspiration in his everyday tools. His ideas travel with him when he is riding his bike, when he is sitting at his desk, when he is tackling a different project. Working on design and machining is what actually provides Bob with the inspiration he needs to keep going. "You have to give yourself the freedom to go down the rabbit hole, because you never know what you're going to find at all. If you say no, you're doing yourself a disservice. Good design is about what you don't do as much as what you do."

HOMEWORK

The juxtaposed concepts of stillness of mind and movement intrigued me. I found it curious that Dreamers could take such different approaches to drawing energy and creativity to them. Dreamers set a trap for creativity in such different ways, but they are all able to use these methods to harness their creativity. Sitting and thinking may not work for you, so movement might be a better path to try. Perhaps meditation and breath work really are the secret to unlocking your creativity, or driving or racing cars may help you think, but it may just terrify you.

With so many ways to create a space to think, remember that each of these Dreamers has their own method. They all set about creating a headspace, or have practiced multiple methods of ideation and setting a trap for creativity to understand how to create a headspace that helps them think, whether that is sitting quietly, walking, or driving a car. And each method is quite personal and unique.

You should try different methods like those listed above and begin to listen to your creativity about what works for you.

Walking may work for some but may be too distracting for others. It may also work to clean your creative space, whether an office, a studio, a fire escape—wherever it may be, declutter it. For some, it may be making a cup of coffee first thing in the morning and sitting down to write.

Dan Killian used to book conference rooms at his old office and stay after work for two to three hours to find the time to work on Pricetitution. Bring a creative idea on a plane, train, commute, or on a car trip with you and just plug in and start writing, creating, planning, or taking the next action you need to take. You'll be amazed how much you can accomplish and how easily you can enter a flow state.

The only way to find out what trap works for you and your creative being is to try them all. Some you will immediately know are not for you, and some will work instantly. Others also grow on you and allow you to find yourself slowly through the practice. I often find that Dreamers who exercise find this to be the case. They resist at first, but start to find deeper layers they did not know they could access through exercise. So try some of these methods, or maybe you know that drinking coffee on your couch with a newspaper helps you clear your headspace to enter a creative frame of mind, so do that. Listen to your body and know what works for you.

CHAPTER 9

CREATE YOUR OWN OPPORTUNITY

If you don't write your own script, someone else will write it for you.

—CHASE JARVIS, CEO OF CREATIVELIVE

One of the coolest aspects I learned about Dreamers is that they have an incredible ability to turn jokes into jobs. The more Dreamers I spoke to, the clearer this principle of dreaming became. While some were astute at turning jokes into jobs, I found that all Dreamers were incredibly capable of creating their own opportunity.

Erik Lang made his first documentary by confidently asserting he could deliver on a documentary project for an artist before he really began working with film. Ted Gushue never really planned to keep knocking on doors and finding opportunities, but new opportunities present themselves every day. Max

Büsser made a casual joke over coffee that would land him a job in the watch industry.

You never know where opportunity is going to strike, so be ready in any situation. These creatives have a unique, almost unnatural ability to, in any situation, create their own opportunity. As Erik Lang said, it all comes down to being slightly more curious than you are afraid of failing. Approaching life with this attitude will allow you to find many more opportunities in your daily life.

YOU MAKE IT UP

I asked Ted Gushue how he landed his role as the global cultural ambassador for automotive culture to the town of St. Moritz, Switzerland. His response was: "You don't. You make it up." His voice is deep and upbeat, and he speaks quickly. Every sentence he drops some knowledge on me—and it's not so much about being a creative entrepreneur, but about living life on your own terms. And if Ted Gushue is doing anything, he is living life on his terms and taking the risks he knows he needs to take to be fulfilled. Ted is willing to pay for a ticket to get into the room, and if nothing comes of it, he was happy to go on the ride. Ted is, ultimately, free.

Ted admits that paying to go hang out in St. Moritz was "a really bad business decision," but he never would have landed the job without it. The role is entirely made up. Deciding that one of his bucket list automotive pursuits was the Bernina Gran Turismo, a hill climb for vintage cars up the Bernina

Pass in Switzerland, Ted leaped at an opportunity to go. Ted had an opportunity, and he took the jump. He started working with the event, which gave him access to influencers at the Board of Tourism. That introduction gave Ted an opportunity to attend all the events at the Bernina Gran Turismo, to be in the room with decision-makers, and to have conversations at dinner parties.

As a result, the fake role created for him turned into a real role and a retainer from the Board of Tourism.[64]

Ted's willingness to follow his curiosity led him to conversations that may otherwise never have taken place. These opportunities are hard to quantify and even harder to predict, but if he hadn't taken an opportunity to be there, Ted would never have found this position.

"There's no grand scheme or plan that I am working toward. The analogy I would use is that I keep knocking on doors until one opens, and then that one opened, and then I go into another room with more doors. And then I do it again. And that's the progression of my life. There's been very little grand scheming."

Ted truly embodies the freedom of risk-taking and seems to enjoy, nay, thrive on that chaos of walking on the knife edge of success and failure. But more often than not, Ted walks out ahead of the game. Other country-level tourism boards have contacted him, and he maintains a contract with Porsche

---

64   Gushue and Pulvirent, "Hodinkee Radio Episode 15: Ted Gushue."

Automotive Group to provide their online digital content and run *Type 7*, a Porsche enthusiast magazine.

"I've done everything I have wanted to do, and I get to do it every day."[65] The sincerity with which Ted declares this on his 2019 episode of the Hodinkee Podcast is jaw-dropping. He seems to have attained ultimate clarity and to understand exactly why he is creating. Ted creates to live the lifestyle he wants. I was amazed to hear someone so free as Ted speaking to me on the phone. This chapter will highlight other success stories of creatives making their own luck and demonstrate the importance of creating our own opportunities.

ARE WE REALLY MAKING IT ALL UP AS WE GO?

Creativity doesn't just have to apply to something we might consider in the arts: painting, photography, music, dance, etc. Creativity actually applies to all aspects of our lives, whether that be writing code professionally, consulting for other businesses, developing new products, or analyzing data. Creativity occurs in actually creating our lives and making choices to do what we think is best. And if you haven't been doing that and have been living off someone else's script, the time has come to start writing your own.

Michael A. "Mickey" Singer's *The Surrender Experiment* is an incredible resource for learning what happens when you surrender to what life is telling you. In the book, he recounts his life's work surrendering to the plans of the universe, listening

---

65   Gushue and Pulvirent, "Hodinkee Radio Episode 15: Ted Gushue."

to what was happening around him and where nature was pointing him, and then building businesses around those ideas. He built several major businesses during his life and has had time to publish two books.

He credits much of his ability to surrender to life to his early practice in mediation and trying to quiet the voice inside his head. As he took time to sit and really think about life, he found himself learning more and more about what he was supposed to be doing by turning off his brain. "I am so grateful that surrender had taught me to willingly participate in life's dance with a quiet mind and an open heart."[66] Perhaps this is what most creatives do: surrender to nature's dance and their own creativity, and great things happen.

Dr. Edward A. Wasserman, Ph.D., is a professor of experimental psychology and director of the Comparative Cognition Laboratory at the University of Iowa. In his article "Are We Just Making It Up As We Go Along?" Dr. Wasserman complicates this issue by arguing that humans are not necessarily making up their journey as they go along. While some of life's journey is unscripted, most of life's happenings build on prior experience and past knowledge of a subject, giving us the unique ability to "appreciate the intricate interplay between the façade of spontaneity and the shaping of behavior by its consequences."[67]

---

66 Michael A. Singer, in *The Surrender Experiment* (New York: Random House, 2015), pp. 159-159.

67 Edward A. Wasserman, "Are We Just Making It Up As We Go Along?," *Psychology Today* (Sussex Publishers, June 3, 2019).

Dr. Wasserman argues that we do not fly by the seat of our pants and arrive at success. While we may plan ahead, the uncertainties of life cause us to routinely change or adjust course to meet our original plan. Failure to do so may cause us to deviate from our original planning. Secondly, he argues that current behavior and expectations are informed by past experiences, allowing us to actually build a platform for forecasting future growth and development. Third, our brains continue to develop and evolve to harness knowledge and overcome challenges that the natural course of life may throw in our way, allowing us to adapt to meet the circumstances.

While some people may just appear more creative than others, we know this is simply not the case. We are all born with the same natural creative ability, some are just more practiced at it than others. And while sometimes we clearly have room in our lives for uncertainty and creativity, we always have an element of planning to consider. As Dr. Wasserman points out, our past experiences influence our current actions, and we can always take a risk to create our own opportunities.

LEARNING FROM THE PROS

Ming Thein is a master at reinventing himself and creating his own opportunity. He is a true Renaissance man, graduating with a master's degree from Oxford at sixteen years old. He achieved success in a professional career in private equity and the corporate world, designed aerodynamic parts for

Formula 1 cars, achieved the highest levels of professional photography, and started a watch company. Needless to say, Ming qualifies as a Renaissance man.

Having successfully climbed the ranks through consulting firms, private equity firms, and finally a career at McDonald's on track to be the country head for Malaysia, Ming Thein realized he did not want to keep doing the things his coworkers were doing. A long-time passion for photography, however, provided exactly what he needed: an escape from the corporate world.

Realizing the internet lacked a good resource for unbiased camera reviews that were published quickly, Ming set to buy and review cameras as rapidly as possible after release. He would shoot, research, and write a substantial review as quickly as possible before publishing camera reviews. Ming recognized that, like him, many people were hunting for unbiased reviews of camera equipment.

His reviews, combined with excellent photos and content, would drive traffic. He aimed to be the first to publish a long-form, well-thought-out review. From there, his work grew into educating readers on the elements of photography and how to shoot better photographs. And as the reviews and education sections of the site started to take off, Ming realized he had an opportunity to work with brands as a creative consultant for their digital content, and the third arm of the business was born.

The consulting work Ming did for brands focused on working with watch brands to shoot their new watches, igniting a passion for watches. Once he got the creative itch, Ming couldn't help but turn his business mind to working on building a watch brand and the things he would do differently. With that in mind, a conversation with friends about watches, the watch industry, and what they would do differently quickly became a design sketch, and then a real idea.

Without necessarily intending to, Ming found himself building a design and launching a watch brand. His past partnerships with watch brands had provided him with enough connections to understand which organizations he could work with to develop and build his new watches. The MING brand launched its first watch in 2017 and has been going strong since, winning awards in 2019. If Ming hadn't taken an opportunity when the conversation arose among friends, who knows what would have happened to his brand?

SOMETIMES THE OPPORTUNITY FINDS YOU

While finishing his master's degree in microtechnology engineering, Max Büsser was in the process of interviewing with both Nestle and Procter & Gamble. During the course of his studies, Max became interested in watches and wanted to learn why something mechanical was still in high demand in a time of technology. To learn more, Max wrote to the managing directors of all of the major watch brands based around Geneva and requested an interview with them to learn more about engineering, and how they were still able to sell a mechanical watch.[68]

One of the people Max interviewed was Henry-John Belmont, then CEO of Jaeger LeCoultre. In our interview, Max recalls meeting Mr. Belmont and recalls this being the first time in his entire engineering career "that somebody spoke to my heart, to my guts. And I thought that was so incredible. And didn't realize in the moment why it was incredible until many years later. . . . I just started really falling in love with watchmaking, because it was beautiful, because it was the condensed version of humanity. And it spoke to me, it spoke to my soul, it spoke to everything which was not rational."

During a ski trip with friends to Verbier, Switzerland, in January 1991, Max decided to stop at a café. Henry-John Belmont, the same CEO Max had interviewed earlier in the year, just so happened to be sitting in the same café. Max and Henry-John Belmont began chatting over coffee and caught up about Max's career plans. Max joked that if none of his other jobs worked out, Belmont could offer him a job at Jaeger LeCoultre.[69]

Max recounts on episode twenty-six of the Hodinkee Radio Podcast from January 7, 2019, that a week later, Belmont requested that Max join him at his office. Max went and, after

68 Maximilian Büsser and Stephen Pulvirent, "Hodinkee Radio Episode 26: Maximilian Büsser," Hodinkee Radio Podcast, January 7, 2019, New York City, NY, podcast, 01:08:48.
69 Büsser and Pulvirent, "Hodinkee Radio Episode 26: Maximilian Büsser."

a few hours of conversation, was offered a job. Max thought on it for a little bit and decided to dive in, knowing full well that he was hooked.

"What was incredible was being part of that little gang of people who was actually resuscitating a brand in an era when nobody wanted watchmaking or a mechanical watch. And it was feeling like those crazy rebels in a world of sanity. Everybody is saying you are insane. Everybody looks at you as if you are nuts. But you do it because you love it. And you're trying to save a company and save an industry actually. I think what Jaeger gave me was the sense of meaning, which is what stimulated my creativity."[70] All in, Max would spend more than seven years at Jaeger rebuilding the brand, before a recruiting firm hired him away.

Max had to create his own opportunity and did so by taking on his interest in mechanical watches and using his position as a student to reach out to managing directors and CEOs of watch brands. This step is so critical in the creative journey: connecting with other creatives and opening yourself to learning from them and with them could lead to incredible opportunities down the road. Just like Max joking with Henry-John Belmont that he could always offer Max a job, we have to joke with the universe and our creativity, and we put crazy ideas out there. That's how Max was able to turn a joke into a job and get to work on something he had always dreamed of.

---

70 Büsser and Pulvirent, "Hodinkee Radio Episode 26: Maximilian Büsser."

SHOULD WE ALL JUST MAKE IT UP?

These Dreamers all had opportunities, or even jobs, working for others before they took a chance on their own creativity. In some cases, they still have full-time jobs that help them support their creativity. As these Dreamers moved through their initial phases of work, they kept seeking opportunities, or taking opportunities as they presented themselves. In some cases, they chose the wrong opportunity and quickly realized they needed to work alone to start their own creative project. In other cases, the opportunity was the right one and helped them to grow as a person, as a creative, and develop their sense of self and their creative language.

On the July 22, 2019, episode of the "Blamo! Podcast," Chris Grainger, CEO of IWC Schaffhausen, a watch brand, said, "If you have time to be bored, you have time to be creative."[71] This quote sums up everything about creativity.

You have to make time for creativity. You have to let it come into your life so you can pursue any creative vision or know what creativity you want to bring into the world. And from there, you'll find it extremely easy to make the time and set the trap to bring creativity into your world. Boredom is really the opportunity to create something you want to see in the world; boredom provides the opportunity for creativity. You just have to recognize the boredom, have the willpower to turn off the TV, quit scrolling through your smartphone, and sit down and do the real work of creating an opportunity to bring your vision into the world.

---

71   Chris Grainger and Jeremy Kirkland, "Chris Grainger: CEO of IWC," BLAMO! Podcast, July 22, 2019, 43:51.

HOMEWORK

I am a big fan of writing lists. The experience is somehow so tactile, whether the list is for groceries or a to-do list, and being able to check things off is so satisfying. I think the best place to start creating your own opportunity is to look to your past experience. What work experience do you have? What have you studied? What are you curious enough about that you want to research and work with every day?

These are the places to start looking for ways to create your own opportunity. As you have discussions with friends, family, even strangers in a coffee shop, look for opportunities in those conversations. Look to freelance job sites, listen to your favorite podcasters and writers, reach out to and connect with industry insiders on LinkedIn. Do you have a skill you can offer them? Even if you start for free, that is a good way to get experience and begin building that skill set.

Sometimes we all just have to take a chance, make a poor business decision, and go try something because we want to. Doing so certainly worked out for the Dreamers highlighted in this chapter. Creating your own opportunity is a skill set like creativity, and you have to hone it every day.

CHAPTER 10

EXECUTION IS EVERYTHING

I have no special talents. I am only passionately curious.

—ALBERT EINSTEIN

What did Dreamers do differently from everyone else when creating their own opportunity? They started. They made a plan and then they executed on it. They made a prototype, no matter how rudimentary, and began working from there. They were not afraid to get started—they just began, often in earnest, and that led to improvements, learnings, and usually better products.

In researching these Dreamers, I noted a handful of traits that linked them together:

- Dreamers are not afraid to talk to potential clients, or to ask potential clients if they may be of service. They want to be of service, and they recognize the value of their creativity to potential clients. Dreamers understand how their unique skills, abilities, and personalities add value, and they are willing to wait for the right client to find them.

- Dreamers know their skill set and the value they add. No other individual on the planet shares their unique interests, background, and skills and can add value to clients in the same way they do.

- Dreamers are passionately curious, not only in their given area of expertise, but they are usually multi-interested and curious to learn about new things.

- Dreamers understand that execution is everything. They understand that an idea means nothing without execution, and execution is critical to actually pursuing your creative vision. You have to create the ritual daily, set the trap for creativity, and use it to actually develop your vision and execute it for clients.

The above combination of skills allows Dreamers to generate a sense of fulfillment from working with their own hands, their own mind, to bringing a vision into the world. You need to be able to ask for what you need creatively, whether from a client or from your family, to have space to create. You must also understand how you are adding value and why. Are you adding value to clients by providing a service they are unable to reproduce at home?

Creativity isn't a finite resource. The more things you learn, look at, try, the more you will be able to do and the more these will inform your perspective. What is so cool about creativity is that it is not exclusive to one area of your life. Whether you want to create to support yourself and as a career move, or you just want to create to express your own vision, you have to be unafraid to ask for what you need, add value, and execute on your plan.

NEVER BE AFRAID TO WALK IN AND ASK

Tim Bent loves to find wonderful and quirky Edwardian accessories. His store at 91 Lower Sloane Street is like walking into the office of the most interesting man in the world. Vintage luggage and lighting adorn the shop windows, and leather swivel chairs invite you to sit down. The glass storefront draws in the natural light, while shelves and drawers invite you to explore and open each to see what's inside. Exploring what's next? That's exactly what drives Tim Bent, founder and owner of Bentley's, a specialist vintage shop founded in 1989.[72]

Tim was a different breed when it came to approaching stores. Tim had a willingness to walk into a store, face a potential rejection, and ask if they would like to have a few pieces to enhance the look and feel of their store. This approach often resulted in Tim dragging a pile of suitcases into each of these stores and selling what they liked.

---

72   Tim Bent, "About," Bentleys Antique Shop London, accessed August 2019.

Tim surmised that menswear stores were the most logical places for his look to work, and he set about targeting them and asking if he could help them. In targeting menswear stores, Tim was finding out that "people appreciate exemplary craftsmanship and that is very, very difficult to find now." In essence, Tim was providing a service in sourcing and curating a selection of well-designed, well-built products with unique craftsmanship. As Tim experienced success with selling, he was hungry to keep buying.

When Tim started, the market was limited. "There wasn't really very much market, then it was very much I was buying entirely what I liked. And then trying to find people that that would buy it from me. I would just walk into stores and say, 'Do you fancy having some lovely luggage for your window?' I was quite a passionate salesman with it, because I was doing what I really enjoyed. And I think all the time, I just wanted to find a way to carry on doing what I was really enjoying doing. And so that's good. That's very good motivation. And then it doesn't feel like working at all!"

Ultimately, Tim is doing what he likes and waiting for the rest of us to catch on. Tim offers a great piece of advice in this sentiment. He has found a unique business that he enjoyed building, but ultimately the initial market was small. He said that "I am doing what I like and just wait to find people that like it as well." Tim had patience.

He also had resilience. He received a lot of "no"s in those first years of walking into stores and asking if they wanted some vintage pieces to complement their shop. Tim gets quiet for a moment thinking about how to phrase his advice and tells me that one must have to have belief and resilience if you are going to make it work. You need to believe in the product and why you are doing what you are doing, and you have to have resilience to be told "no" in countless meetings and still believe in the product you are selling and the viability of the marketplace. It will come; every time you hear a "no," you just haven't found the right buyer yet. Tim has also found that, even if business is really tough, working for yourself is the most enjoyable. Tim gathers his thoughts, and in a slow exhalation, he tells me, "I have always found it to be an amazing freedom."

Tim Bent is a great example of the four principles demonstrated by Dreamers. First, Tim is never afraid to walk in and ask a potential customer if he can add value. Second, Tim knows not only the value that he provides to customers, but also the value that his products bring to a customer. Tim has the added bonus of having the patience to wait for the right buyer. Third, Tim is extremely curious to find his next purchase and lives for the thrill of hunting down additions for his collection, even though letting go of fantastic finds is sometimes painful. He is always excited about what's next. Finally, Tim just got started. While still in school, Tim was selling vintage clothes, and he kept his faith in his skills and his vision and kept working toward it.

THE DREAMER'S PURSUIT

In his words, Tim likes to buy what he likes and is willing to wait for the right customer. So why wouldn't you create what you want and wait for the world to catch up? It always comes down to the willingness of the Dreamer to take action.

Ming Thein, photographer, camera reviewer, and now watch brand owner from Chapter 8, wanted to get out of the corporate world and pursue his goal by beginning to write and shoot photographs. He dreamed of starting a camera review site that provided unbiased reviews and didn't stop until he found his voice, which led him to be a leading expert and go-to resource for camera reviews on the internet.

Ming worked hard to get his website going, which led to offering education for photographers, shooting commercially, and working for Hasselblad, a camera company, as chief of strategy. As a commercial photographer, Ming was able to use his passion for photography to actually help his clients with creative direction and strategy. Working with watch brands ignited a passion that would occupy Ming's mind for a long time to come.

He was frustrated by some of the things he felt were missing from the watch industry. He saw an element of caring for the customer, providing little details like travel pouches and extra watch straps, and interchangeability within the product line that wasn't available within the industry. Recognizing these issues, Ming and some friends decided they would take on a new project: building a watch brand. He sat down to get to work on a design direction, and the watch brand MING was launched in 2017.

Ming makes the point that if you are good enough at something and loud enough about it, people will find you. Ming is willing to pursue potential customers, and he has no issues talking to media or looking for media coverage; however, Ming is willing to wait for the watch industry and watch aficionados to come to his brand. Ming makes the point that we should be loud about our creative pursuits, and who knows, what starts as a personal creative project might become something much larger. For Ming, working in the corporate world made him want to seek a more creative project, which led him to building his own watch brand. He sat down, decided he wanted to pursue this work, and executed on his vision.

EXECUTION IS EVERYTHING

I have often felt the desire to be creative and have started down the path of many projects. I begin the project with a ton of enthusiasm to attack it and build something from it. But a few weeks in, I find myself lacking an understanding of what it actually takes to execute on that plan. I lose focus or don't understand where to go next. I have found that pursuing something simply as a curiosity helps to take the pressure off, and I tend to get more done or be more focused on pursuing the work if I don't put too much pressure on it.

I didn't realize I needed to shift my mindset on creative pursuits until I sat down to talk with Dan Killian. He and I have ended up in very similar places working for other people, yet Dan was able to turn on his creativity and actually use the time he was at his job to influence the creation of his game Pricetitution.

As we talk about the process of bringing his game to life, Dan tells me that "execution is everything." Dan continues that "staying in the safe space of ideating and hiding" isn't actually helping you move a creative project forward. To actually bring your project into the world, you need to get started. Dan's advice? "Get out there and prototype something as fast as you possibly can. And you can do that in two hours." Dan again closes this train of thought with the adage "execution is everything."

And I began to realize that Dan was absolutely right. For each of my thirty-two ideas, I could invest two hours into each business, write a business plan canvas, and see how much I am invested in the business and share that with a few friends to get some feedback. A simple solution to start narrowing things down. I had also seen this approach while working in software: often we just had to prototype something to see if it would work, to move forward from the idea phase into execution.

Progressing from idea to execution is hard. Gaining and building momentum is tricky, especially as we start to resist the closer something is to us, or the more near and dear to our hearts, because as humans we don't want to manage the heartbreak that may accompany the failure of this idea. The deeply personal nature of creative work can hold us back from actually putting our nascent ideas out into the world. In our heads, the ideas are perfect, totally executable, and all definitely good ideas. On paper and in execution, they may be totally different.

As Dan said, prototype *something*. That first step will start to give you ideas, help you solicit feedback, and develop the concept. Prototype again, and see if it works. Sometimes it won't. In fact, more often than not, it won't. And that is the scariest part of creativity. The deeply personal nature, the personal connection we have to our ideas, makes us feel tied to them, and their success or failure determines our personal success or failure. That is a limiting belief that Dreamers let go of a long time ago.

The success or failure of an idea does not determine your success or failure in your own life. Creatives like Sheena, Max, Ted, Dan, Ming, and Tim all let go of that idea long ago. They are creating for themselves because doing so is fun, and the fact that their work resonates with so many people is awesome. It will never resonate with everyone, so stop trying to please everyone. And the only way to start finding your audience is to start executing on your vision now. That could be twenty minutes per day, or it could be all-in, quitting your job and running with it. That is for you to decide. But you cannot build an audience until you execute on your idea, prototype something, and bring your vision into the world.

CREATING FOR THE CUSTOMER

George Glasgow Jr. is the CEO of British bespoke shoemaker George Cleverley. George speaks to me over a coffee from a café in Mayfair and tells me that he recognizes no one genuinely needs his products. But that is not the point. For him, the point of delivering a traditional bespoke handmade shoe to a customer is the relationships the customer builds with their shoes.

And George finds it interesting not only to hear customer's stories of where their shoes take them, but getting to create new styles, test new products, and understand what the response is within the market. And George is certainly no stranger to executing a business vision. Before George joined the business, he worked in the workshop during holidays from school and during weekends. He learned all aspects of the business, which helped him become more creative in learning all aspects of the business. George also visits tanneries and helps clients order new combinations of materials or new colors, which allows George to ask tanneries to create new color ways and lets George develop new styles. Making pairs of shoes for himself allows George to prototype the shoe, show it to people, and solicit feedback, helping boost his creativity by essentially prototyping with new materials.

Knowing what he likes helps him understand what his customers will like. Sourcing new materials and colors allows George's creativity to play with new ideas and combinations, challenge tradition, and push the envelope ever so slightly with some of his work. George also finds that customers come to him with an idea and then he is set on a creative path to help them develop the style and find the perfect combination of materials or even develop new materials for shoes.

George entirely understands what it takes to actually execute a business plan. By being his own customer, he gets to play with ideas, styles, and colors and beta-test new ideas, allowing him to add value to his customers by generating ideas, devising new ways to wear shoes, and making his products an indispensable part of a gentleman's wardrobe. He is also never afraid to show a customer a new product or design and solicit their feedback, helping him understand the market and refine products. By keeping his finger so close to the pulse of his customer, George is able to anticipate customer needs before they arise.

HOMEWORK

To figure out how to execute, you need to take your creative vision and break it down into tangible pieces. You could start by asking yourself questions about the vision, including "why?" or "how?" and start trying things. A business planning canvas might be the best place to start. Never be afraid to start asking customers, readers, whomever for feedback and information, and see if you can develop a relationship.

To add value, you have to understand your creative vision, where you sit in the market, and how relevant you are to that marketplace. Adding value, to me, is an extension of execution. You have to understand your skills, strengths, and unique outlook, and translate that into why you need to pursue this work and why someone else should listen. By putting your vision out into the world and being loud about it, people who resonate with your vision will find you.

I keep coming back to Dan Killian's advice: just prototype something. It could be made with a sheet of printer paper. It doesn't have to be fancy, you just need to start working on it and getting the ideas out of your head and into the world so you can continue to develop them, and then relatively quickly determine if it is something that will add value or if you need to make changes. Rapid prototyping also allows access to creativity, as you can prototype different versions and test and retest to see what resonates with friends, family, and potential customers.

CHAPTER 11

CURIOSITY IS CREATIVITY

———

The cure for boredom is curiosity. There is no cure for curiosity.

—DOROTHY PARKER

Dreamers are curious people who look for opportunity in every area of their life. Dreamers are always looking for a way to turn their curiosity into creativity and opportunities where it may not have previously been. One thing I certainly learned from Dreamers is that curiosity is a form of creativity. You need to follow it wherever it leads and see where it takes you.

Dreamers are fantastic at following their curiosities and turning jokes into jobs.

Max Büsser turned his curiosity about the watch industry and why mechanical watches were still a viable business in an age of technology into a job. During his studies, Max reached out to the managing directors of major watch brands and was lucky enough to meet the CEO of Jaeger LeCoultre, Mr. Henry-John Belmont. After their discussion, Max left understanding more about the watch industry, with no intention of joining.

Max ran into Mr. Belmont at a ski resort in Switzerland, and Max gave him an update on his job search. At that meeting, Max quipped that if both P&G and Nestle failed to hire him, Mr. Belmont could offer him a job at Jaeger. Max was invited to interview and given the job. Max wasn't even considering entering the watch industry for work.

This notion is in complete juxtaposition to what he tells the crowd gathered for his talk at Salon International de la Haute Horlogerie Genève, Geneva's watch fair showcasing the works of the best and brightest in the industry. Max calmly tells the crowd, with the slightest crack in his voice, that "watchmaking saved my life."[73] Watchmaking means a great deal to Max and taking a chance to make a joke about working alongside Henry-John Belmont landed Max the job that would help to launch his future.

TURNING CURIOSITY INTO CREATIVITY
Speaking to me from a café in Italy, Ted Gushue is as animated as the background noise. His voice is deep and upbeat, and he speaks quickly. With each sentence, you can hear his

---

73   *SIHH2019: You Never Lose: You Win – Or You Learn /
      by MB&F, YouTube* (MB&F, 2019).

enthusiasm for creative pursuits and his positivity that the world we currently inhabit is the most creative-friendly world we have ever seen. I wanted to find out how Ted pursues his creativity and where he seems to find his boundless energy for creating content and beautiful photographs to share with the world.

Ted laughs and I can almost hear him shrugging when he sheepishly admits, "I just follow my nose, kind of, accept opportunities that in many cases would be inadvisable but have led to real opportunities." Ted has always followed his curiosity, and that curiosity has helped him continue to find opportunities.

Direly wanting to participate in the Bernina Gran Turismo, a classic car hill climb up the Bernina Pass in St. Moritz, Switzerland, Ted admits that going to the Bernina Gran Turismo and "paying my way to go to hang out in St. Moritz is a really bad business decision."[74] By being present, Ted was able to meet folks from the St. Moritz Tourism Board and develop relationships there. "Because I was in the room, and because I was having the conversations and at the dinner parties, they created a fake role. That turned into a real role. Now I have an annual retainer from the town of St. Moritz."

Ted continues to follow his curiosity wherever it will lead him. With an interest in all things motorsport, Ted explores all facets of the motorsport world. His advice is to just keep knocking on doors of opportunities and keep trying. Much

---

74   Gushue and Pulvirent, "Hodinkee Radio Episode 15: Ted Gushue."

like we learned from Tim Bent, an audience exists out there for your creative project. You may just have to wait for the right audience to come along.

LIVING A CURIOSITY-DRIVEN LIFE

In an article appearing in *HuffPost* titled "Why Curiosity Is the Key to Breakthrough Creativity," Andrew Merle explores why curiosity is so critical to actually developing creativity. "If you want to live a curiosity-driven life, you must commit to being vigilant about looking for what's piquing your curiosity."[75] Merle points out that Liz Gilbert is a big believer that following your curiosity, rather than your passion, leads to living an interesting life.

According to the article, following your curiosity allows you to actually approach "uncertainty with a positive attitude— relaxing and opening our minds to new ideas, skills, and ways of solving problems."[76] In an age of representing perfection on social media, we often look for one overarching thing that we can be the best at. But it is completely okay to approach something as a novice and just be interested in it for the sake of being curious without needing to be the best at it.

This idea falls in line with the research we saw from Dr. Land— children pursue curiosity with a dogged determination and don't stop asking questions. But as an adult we are fearful

---

75 Andrew Merle, "Why Curiosity Is The Key To Breakthrough Creativity," HuffPost (HuffPost, December 7, 2017).

76 Merle, "Why Curiosity Is The Key To Breakthrough Creativity."

of being judged or being less than our peers and not understanding something. And that is the exact barrier we need to break through. Unlocking your curiosity will help unlock your creativity. It's giving yourself permission to explore as many possibilities as you want and then moving forward.

Merle suggests that researching is a form of curiosity, and I completely agree.[77] I often get so wrapped up in researching something I am just learning about that I lose track of time, completely entering a flow state. If something is a curiosity that doesn't completely envelop you, that's fine too! It's important to pay attention to your intuition and what it is telling you as you progress in exploring your creativity.

QUESTION WHY YOU ARE INTRIGUED

Author Amy Tan's 2008 TEDx Talk titled "Where Does Creativity Hide?" ponders whether creativity is a neurological quirk or just what drives us to be creative beings. She argues that part of curiosity and creativity are born of identity crisis: understanding "Who am I and why am I this particular person?"[78] Tan comes up with three central questions she wanted to explore: "Why do things happen? How do things happen? How do I make things happen?"[79]

Tan argues that you want to find a synergy between ideas, and you ultimately "want to find what matters." She goes on

---

77 Merle, "Why Curiosity Is The Key To Breakthrough Creativity."

78 Amy Tan, *Where Does Creativity Hide?*, *TED2008* (TED, 2008).

79 Amy Tan, *Where Does Creativity Hide?*, *TED2008* (TED, 2008).

to say that while writing one of her books, she found things that had been quite obvious in her life. She argues that moral ambiguity is such a challenging thing for humans, yet so necessary to actually be a human and live a life. Tan arrives at the point of "how do I build my own life?"

Amy Tan is of the stringent belief that you arrive at how to build your own life by questioning. Tan argues that you will never find complete answers to any question posed to the universe. Rather, "there is uncertainty in everything, and that is good because I will discover something new."[80] To write a successful work, she has to become the uncertainty within her stories to discover something of the thread that runs through her life.

Curiosity is fueled not only by the life we wish to live, but the life we currently live. Look at the life around you and look to your dream life. You might just find out something more is there that coincides and helps you develop a true reality upon which you can build your story.

THE CURIOSITY QUOTIENT

Amy Tan's questioning view of why you are the person you are is representative of your curiosity. To understand it further, you need to get curious about your own life. Tomas Chamorro-Premuzic works for ManPower Group and writes for *Harvard Business Review* and researches the Curiosity Quotient. Intelligence Quotient, or IQ, measures a person's

---

80 Amy Tan, *Where Does Creativity Hide?*, TED2008 (TED, 2008).

naturally intellectual capability, while the Curiosity Quotient, or CQ, measures how "hungry" your mind is for new information.[81]

What Chamorro-Premuzic found intrigued me. "CQ leads to higher levels of intellectual investment and knowledge acquisition over time, especially in formal domains of education, such as science and art."[82] This finding reinforces the idea that it is okay to simply be curious for knowledge about something. You do not have to invest tons of time and energy, but that interest, that spark of curiosity in and of itself, is important. It means your mind is seeking new and more information.

That desire to seek new information, to add domain experience and expertise to your toolkit, can only serve to make you more creative. Chamorro-Premuzic continues his argument that "knowledge and expertise, much like experience, translate complex situations into familiar ones, so CQ is the ultimate tool to produce simple solutions for complex problems."[83] This idea suggests that the more we learn, the easier it is to make unfamiliar situations feel normal, which translates well for creativity. The more time you invest in a creative project, the simpler it gets and the more easily you can acquire new information or became creative in different aspects of your life.

81 Tomas Chamorro-Premuzic, "Curiosity Is as Important as Intelligence," Harvard Business Review, November 5, 2014.
82 Tomas Chamorro-Premuzic, "Curiosity Is as Important as Intelligence."
83 Tomas Chamorro-Premuzic, "Curiosity Is as Important as Intelligence."

Curiosity is clearly and inextricably linked to creativity. Curiosity allows you to approach problems with a positive attitude and outlook without putting so much pressure on yourself. You have to explore new areas of study or new things you want to learn about with curiosity rather than force. Curiosity can temper your expectations of outcomes, helping you pursue a curiosity or a creative project simply for the joy of doing it.

CURIOSITY VS. PASSION

I personally find "follow your passion" to be terrible advice and greatly appreciate the idea of following your curiosities. I am curious about so many things that I initially had great difficulty determining what I actually wanted to do. The advice to follow your passion is so much easier to use because passion, in that sentence, is presented as a singular item, not as a plural, which implies it should be easier because you should simply have one overarching passion to follow. And I just have to say, following just one passion or thread is flawed logic.

Chasing your curiosity is much more interesting. Curiosity leads to discoveries and subjects that you might have had no idea existed. Let curiosity be the guide, and if your interest is piqued, use passion to propel your research and chase down every last thread of information. In college I found myself interested in astronomy and took every class available to me as an astronomy novice and someone who was never going to major in physics or in astronomy. I was just curious about it. I deeply wanted to understand the world around me.

This topic reminds me of something Ted Gushue told me. "If you're willing to do it for free, you'll be very successful at it." I started to wonder how true this was. It is common practice for college students to take on unpaid internships for credit, but I am not sure those are the most rewarding gigs. I started to think about this quote more and more and what it meant. I am not sure Ted meant it in the literal sense of whatever job you have and would do for free full time, or if rather by doing it for free you are building a passion, curiosity, and an ability to do that work.

That is the crux of what you should be looking for in daily life. What makes you tick? What interests you? Where is your free time spent? Find the items in your daily life, the conversation topics that bring you to life, make you tick and find ways to have more and more of those conversations, or time to focus and research. In the next section we are going to learn from creatives who followed their curiosity as it led them to their current work.

REAL-LIFE EXAMPLES

Eric Wind is a tremendous real-life example of following your creativity. Eric is the owner and operator of Wind Vintage, a vintage watch specialist company, buying, selling, and trading watches. Eric became interested in watches because of his grandfather's Hamilton watch, a gift from his grandmother to his grandfather for their wedding. Eric later received it as a birthday present, sparking a curiosity in him to explore the world of watches.

Finding Hodinkee, a watch enthusiast website, Eric voraciously read every post and sought more information. Eric found himself on eBay and other platforms searching for vintage watches and sending them to the editors at Hodinkee to showcase on the site. In addition, Eric began researching and writing his own articles on watches, also submitting them to Hodinkee for publication.

Eric quickly became a regular contributor to Hodinkee. Before he knew it, Eric was writing Hodinkee's "Bring a Loupe" column every week. This column is dedicated to finding unique watches for sale online and presenting research about the watches and links to where readers could find and purchase the watch. "Some of the 'Bring a Loupe' columns were as long as thirty watches or more and would take twenty to thirty hours to do, so I'd be doing it every evening. I was paying my dues and I didn't even know it."

Writing every night after work, looking at eBay to scout for watches, and scouring the depths of the internet for interesting pieces fueled Eric's creativity. He loved the process of looking for watches, learning, and then being able to relay that information to potential future owners. "I like the research. I like trying to grow the market of those interested in watches."

Writing for Hodinkee led Eric to a position at the Christie's auction house, where he focused on overseeing the New York auctions, evaluating watches for sale, and providing scholarship on watches for Christie's globally. During this period, Eric was able to build on his existing knowledge and really hone in on the vintage watches he loved. Eric used this knowledge to build his own business, specializing in selling and sourcing vintage watches.

Eric's advice about following your curiosity is to "learn everything you can. Because knowledge is definitely power and what will separate you from others and what will give you your competitive advantage." And to do that, Eric simply uses his curiosity to ask questions about watches and seek the answers. Eric's curiosity has helped him build his own business, which fuels his interest and creativity to keep finding new watches and meeting new people.

CREATE BECAUSE YOU LOVE TO

Bob Isaac is the perfect example of a creative who is simply curious and wanted to see what he could create, even with a limited set of tools. Bob is an architect and industrial designer who is curious about all things design. One of the first projects he worked on out of school was the Sony Walkman. He fondly remembers sitting in conference rooms, sketching on Post-it Notes, working with a team to find the right combination of ideas. And that same curiosity to find the right combination of ideas drives Bob today.

Bob is a full-time working architect but operates his creative studio Baughb Labs to create things he is interested in. Bob is curious about pens, watches, and mechanical items that we use in our everyday lives. While changing the ink cartridge in his favorite Parker pen, Bob had an idea.

Holding the ink cartridge in his hand, Bob said to himself, "I can make a pen."

No stranger to building with metal, Bob had been creating with and shaping metal for a long time. The first project he tackled was making a CD display tray with only a hacksaw and a file. When the Apple Watch was released, Bob wanted to design and produce a beautiful stand for the watch that would pair well with the design of the watch. Designing all the components and drafting the design, Bob realized he would need to outsource the production, as it was too complicated for him to produce in-house.

Dissatisfied with having to outsource any part of his project, Bob set about learning how to machine on his own. Working on a design project for a friend, Bob bartered his time working on the architectural design for a metal lathe from eBay. Bob had not spent any appreciable time on a metal lathe machine, but he wanted to learn. YouTube videos were a tremendous help, and he was soon using the lathe in his apartment to turn metal into beautiful pieces of functional art.

Bob was simply curious to see if he could actually make something on the lathe and remove the outsourcing of labor on his products. Now that Bob had the ability to produce his products in-house, he returned to the idea of his pen. He drew a sketch of his ideal pen and sketched it again. Next, he used computer-aided design, or CAD, software to draft the pen in a three-dimensional rendering and set about making a prototype. The process of creating a product from an idea in his mind, translating it to paper, making it three-dimensional, and then bringing it to life through a lathe in his apartment spoke to his head, his heart, and his hands. He loved the process and precision of machining metal. And once he started, he just didn't stop.

Bob has made a series of pens and watch tools and continues to ideate and think of new ways in which he can use his metalworking skill. His simple curiosity for learning taught him how to machine and improve his metal-turning skill. Creating beautiful, simple, functional products continues to drive his curiosity. Bob doesn't create for other people or to do this as a full-time job. He simply creates for himself to settle his own curiosity and have the satisfaction of manufacturing entirely in-house.

HOMEWORK
For a start, really pay attention to your dreams and daydreams and where they are pointing you. This is the true magic of dreaming—once you start, you will not be able to stop, and that momentum is the most fun part about being a Dreamer. Every single thing that you look at is an opportunity for the right curious mind. If you start to dream about something, get curious.

I'll repeat that again: BE CURIOUS! Try your hand at every opportunity offered to you. Let your curiosity guide you and let it build skills and confidence, and in turn you will become incredibly well versed in the subject—potentially even the expert! And that aspect is the fun of being a Dreamer, sinking into your curiosity and exploring what the world has to offer. You don't have to invent something new to explore a curiosity, but curiosity often leads to innovation.

Research is where the rubber meets the road of creativity. If your curiosity is really pointing you to research something, go all in. You can spend hours researching, finding a flow state and really sinking into working on something for the sake of learning something new. The funny thing is, this research often leads to a discovery. Curiosity is what has brought us countless innovations. Curiosity discovered that we were not at the center of the universe. Curiosity discovered electricity. Curiosity has genuinely kept innovation moving forward.

Build your curiosity muscles by exploring what intrigues you. You never know what creative insight you are going to unlock.

Once you start using it, creativity never goes away. It is always with you and always there ready for you to jump in and start back where you left off. Curiosity is a great way to engage with your creativity and to create something or think up a dream, even in your head, even if just for yourself. That is the magic of creativity: once you start, you just won't be able to stop.

APPLICATIONS

CHAPTER 12

WHERE TO?

———

Make the most of your regrets; never smother your sorrow, but tend and cherish it till it comes to have a separate and integral interest. To regret deeply is to live afresh.

—HENRY DAVID THOREAU

So here we are. You've seen the way Dreamers unlock their creativity. You have some of their tricks, tactics and methods for creating daily, retaining that creativity, and producing what they want, for themselves and for their customers. What surprised me the most in this process was it didn't lead me where I thought it would.

When I began this book, I thought speaking to all these Dreamers would lead me down a path to an answer of which one of the thirty-two companies that I had dreamt up I would start. I believed I would clearly have an answer and be ready to start a company as soon as my manuscript was turned in.

I was wrong.

What I did learn is that creativity comes in many flavors, and you can find many reasons to create and things from which to draw inspiration. I learned that I get inspiration from time spent in nature. I also learned that it is okay to look for creative pursuits just for yourself, not for anyone else, and not to turn them into a business. Sometimes creating for yourself is all you need.

The biggest takeaway for me is that, to have the freedom and the creativity to pursue multiple curiosities, I need to create my own business. I have not yet found the right combination, but writing this book has provided me the inspiration and habits I need to get there, and most of all, speaking to Dreamers I respect has motivated me. I hope this book serves as an inspiration for you as well.

THE PRINCIPLES OF DREAMING
No matter where you are in the creative journey, the time has come to get started. I give you permission to create whatever you want to bring into this world. I ask that you give yourself permission and get started. Start by creating for yourself. It's not only a great way to interact with your creativity, but also a great way to take the creative pressure off the process and make it something fun to try your hand at.

I often think about what Ellen Bennett said on "The Nitty Gritty Podcast" that she broke down every decision, action, or task into its component pieces. "Business, however complicated it may seem, is comprised of a ton of tiny little actions."[84] Creativity is no different; you have to break a creative project down into component pieces and tackle them one by one.

Every Dreamer is more curious to learn something than they are afraid to fail. This is the attitude you need to cultivate to pursue creativity. Being more curious than you are afraid to fail flips the narrative of self-doubt on its head. Instead of being worried about looking foolish, you become excited to look foolish as an opportunity to learn. Making this approach a routine part of your day will make it easier to ultimately start a creative project and pursue it, because you will know the exact moments in life when you need to choose curiosity over fear.

First, in choosing curiosity over fear, you have to look at how you are using your time. You have to catalog how you are spending the twenty-four hours of your day and understand where in your schedule you can fit in time for creativity. Looking at your schedule will help you find those times to create and times to choose curiosity over fear, to make a change and stick with it, because time is our most precious resource.

Next, you need to find time to design your dream life and develop the end-goal of your creative project by writing a dream essay. Take twenty to thirty minutes to start sketching out your dream life and how creativity fits into it. Think about what your day looks like. What are you doing? Who are you spending time with? Where are you living? Start outlining every detail of your

---

84 Bennett and Haber, "The Nitty-Gritty Podcast: Hedley & Bennett," 5:36.

life, and the more granular you can be, the stronger your essay will be and the more it will propel you toward creativity and building a creative life that you want to live. Plan out a weekend or evening when you do not have other commitments. Turn off your phone, turn off the TV, and get busy dreaming.

Write the outline by hand and the first draft by hand as well, allowing you to use the tactility of writing to enhance the vision and really create a connection to the dream and your goals. Start writing, take action, and just start dreaming. Let that guide how you develop the essay, and look at those gaps in your schedule and use that time to create.

From there, try the methods of setting a trap for creativity that Dreamers like Max, Ted, Sheena, Ming, and Dan use to bring creativity into their lives daily. Try as many combinations as possible. Try stillness, try movement, try opening a word processor and writing down every idea that pops into your head, go for a walk in nature, design something for a potential customer, design something that only you want. All these methods work for Dreamers, and you may find a unique way to combine the methods that helps you to set a trap for creativity. Create your own ritual.

Get curious about where you draw your inspiration from. This book has significantly reinforced how important daily time in nature is for me. It allows me to contemplate, to walk, to feel grounded and connected to the world around me. This time is sacred to me and I have set an intention of getting time in nature daily.

While setting a trap for creativity, look at what thoughts are recurring, look at the blank space in your day, and see how you are using that free time. What themes repeat and what are you curious to learn about? Chase that curiosity wherever it may lead you. As Ted Gushue said, keep opening doors and enter another room full of doors and just keeping knocking on doors until you find the right opportunity. Go explore whatever you are curious about. You have no guarantee that it will turn into a business, but exploration is part of the creative journey.

This chase will allow you to begin creating your own opportunity, whether that is declaring that you will write a book or suggesting that you might be able to help someone with a documentary film project. With a trap set for creativity, start looking for opportunity. Start looking for jokes you could turn into jobs. This is where Dreamers shine in their ability to turn almost any situation into an opportunity.

Finally, you just have to get started. As we learned from Dreamers in Chapter 11, execution is everything, and if you have an idea, waiting for the right time is a poor strategy—the timing is never going to be right. I always call back to Dan Killian's point that you should prototype something today. Even if it is on a Post-it Note or made out of newspaper, prototyping today will get you started.

If you don't have an idea, I hope you get curious about things you spend your time doing and start to unravel why they are interesting to you. If you don't feel like you have any hobbies, observe what you are looking at on the internet or on social media. Do you feel a calling inside to just try those things? Take a look around—curiosity is a form of creativity. Get out there and find something to be curious about and try to chase down your curiosity.

WHAT DID I LEARN IN WRITING THIS BOOK?

Writing this book, or any other book, was never on the list of the thirty-two companies I wanted to start. I was asked if I wanted to go on this journey by Georgetown University professor Eric Koester, and I just sat down and got started. I was never sure where the book was going, and it has taken a completely different form than what I imagined when we started, but the book is better for it.

I set out to interview these Dreamers and understand their creative process: why they create, how they create, and how they built their own business. I learned that these Dreamers have serious daily habits for setting themselves up for success, setting a trap for creativity, and they do so in many different ways. But they all work on something creative daily. I learned that I needed to build better habits around my creativity. I needed to find a way to set the trap for creativity, get out of my own way, and let creativity flow.

I learned that every Dreamer has their own route to pursuing creativity. No two pursue creativity in the same way; they each have their own unique style that works for them. They had to develop these habits and look at where they were able to change things and what they needed to do to get started with creativity.

All these Dreamers started somewhere. They either found themselves working on creative projects or stuck in a job where they couldn't apply their creativity or be creative in a way that was meaningful to them. Some of these Dreamers would never find a position within a company that allowed them the freedom and risk-taking they enjoy as a solo entrepreneur, though that comes with significant risk. But that also allows them to live life on their terms, and seeing people so free is incredibly inspiring.

The most important lesson I learned in researching this book is that I was not alone in the camp of regret. I learned that I may have thirty-two regrets, and I may have more. No creative path is trending positive at all times. All these Dreamers have struggled at one point or another, but as Winston Churchill once said, "Success is not final, failure is not fatal; it is the courage to continue that counts." I will continue searching until I find the idea that resonates with me the most and that I cannot shake. And then I will pursue it.

I have encountered tremendous resources for anyone who wants to become more creative: podcasts, books, classes, masterclasses, YouTube. These resources can help you pinpoint creativity and continue to drive yourself where you would like to go. Listening to other creators' stories, I was able to really relate to them and understand where they were coming from. The podcasts "How I Built This" from NPR and

"The Business of Hype" from HYPEBEAST are tremendous resources to listen to Dreamers speak about their creative journeys, helping you think of additional ways in which to apply your creativity.

Ted Gushue told me during our interview that we are living in the golden era for creatives and creativity. Startup costs are at an all-time low, and the cost to begin a project has never been lower, which makes taking the leap a lot less risky than starting a creative project has been in the past. All it takes to set up a creative project these days is the cost to start a webpage and the time you need to gather your thoughts. Jump. Get started. Don't wait. Go out into the world and start creating the project and the life you have always dreamed of living.

WHERE AM I GOING?

Having taken on my first serious creative project, I look forward to starting another. I have some ideas for a second book and would love to pursue those ideas. I am also using some of the creative ideas I learned from the Dreamers I interviewed to reevaluate my list of thirty-two regrets. Are these truly regrets, or are they dreams uniquely suited for someone other than me?

This endeavor has been challenging and has shown me some of my core competencies and exposed some of my weaknesses. But writing this book has awakened my interest in research and writing—and connected me with my need to create.

Connecting ideas and presenting them for the reader is very creative for me. I tremendously enjoyed finding research and writing each chapter of this book. The interviews were especially enjoyable, and I left every one feeling completely excited about what was to come. I am also grateful for the opportunity to research and write. I have so frequently lost track of time while interviewing, writing, and researching, and I often came out feeling exhausted but energized.

There is something in this for me, and I plan to unlock more of it with my thirty-third idea. I look forward to beginning the journey of writing a second book.

For a long time, even in high school, I told people I wanted to be a photojournalist. I have always loved photography, but I have always been scared to showcase my work. I have decided that for me, photography, for the time being, is a hobby without the need to put a ton of pressure on it for it to become my job. It is honestly just something I love to do, especially film photography. And that is very fulfilling, to have a hobby that isn't for work or making money. It's a creative project, just for me.

I want to do more research and more writing. I am going to start with a revised business plan for my idea to use drones for avalanche mitigation and victim recovery. Revising that business plan, bringing new innovations and new ideas to solving problems that once stumped me, seems like a good challenge. I feel that I now have a toolkit of actions I can use to make sure this attempt, if not successful, is more structured, and I know what I need to execute on to be successful.

WHAT SHOULD YOU TAKE AWAY FROM THIS BOOK?

I hope you have learned some of the tips, tactics, and techniques that Dreamers use to bring creativity into their lives daily, and I hope this book has helped you understand if creativity is something you need in your life, or an addiction you need to feed daily. My most sincere hope is that you gained some knowledge from this book about how Dreamers pursue their work and why they pursue that work, and that these stories inspire you to get started.

I hope you start a creative project of your own. Success for this book, to me, is helping you to increase your daily creative output and explore creativity and curiosity more deeply. If I was able to help you find a way to build a daily creative practice, that outcome is the most I could ask for.

Whatever you decide to create, I hope you get started. Don't wait for the perfect moment; that moment is now. As we learned from the Dreamers, you may not find a market for your creativity yet, but people will come around. People will become interested if you remain interested in pursuing creativity in the face of a thousand "no"s. Start small, creating for yourself, but get started.

I genuinely hope this book was helpful in you setting a daily creative practice, to take that hobby and dial up the volume on it, and understand that it can be a successful business. If you don't want your creative outlet to become a business, you don't have to create for anyone else. You can create for yourself, and that is totally fine. If you want to create, you just have to make the time and get started.

LEARNING TAKEAWAYS

Perhaps the most important takeaway from this book is that reclaiming your creativity is hard. That doesn't mean you shouldn't give it every effort you have. As we learned from these Dreamers, you can certainly transition from a world of regretting to a world of dreaming, but you are the only one who can get you moving in the right direction.

Sometimes you are going to have to make it up as we go along. Dreamers are really, really talented at turning jokes into jobs. They are able to suggest crazy ideas or say, "Someday I would love to do that," and put the idea out there. In many of the cases of Dreamers I interviewed, this has given them a project or brought their original project to life.

Dreamers are intensely curious people, and I would argue that to be more creative, you simply need to get curious. Remember the words of IWC CEO Chris Grainger: "If you have time to be bored, you have time to be creative."[85]

THE BEGINNING IN AN END

So here we are. You've seen the way Dreamers unlock their creativity. I've learned a lot through this process, but what surprised me the most was it didn't lead me where I thought it would. It led me to creating a project I never thought I would take on and allowed me to speak to some of the most interesting people I have ever had the pleasure of meeting.

---

85   Grainger and Kirkland, "Chris Grainger: CEO of IWC."

The thirty-two company ideas that I had never included writing a book. The book was an ancillary benefit of wanting to understand how to unlock my creativity. I was on a quest to create something—and what better place to start than to write a book on creativity and get to create something I loved?

I hope you complete the homework assignments in this book and genuinely use them to discover a creative process that works for you, and even an abridged version that allows you to get into a creative mindset faster and tackle projects in your professional and personal life.

Whatever you do, you'll find no limit to what you can create, just what your mind allows you to create. Let's backtrack to that inner five-year old and remove the limits of your thinking, start expanding that view, and create. Create something you have always wanted to bring into the world, or explore ideas until you find something that you personally need to create. And keep doing that.

As Howard Thurman said: "Don't ask what the world needs. Ask yourself what makes you come alive, and go do that, because what the world needs is people who have come alive." I hope you find something that makes you come alive, and I hope you share it with the world.

ACKNOWLEDGMENTS

———

I would like to thank everyone who made this book possible. A special thanks to Georgetown professor Eric Koester and the entire team at New Degree Press. Thank you for getting me interested in this project and helping me to see it through.

I would like to thank each of the Dreamers I interviewed to make this book a possibility. Thank you for taking the time to speak to me, telling me your story, and entrusting me with it. In order of interview, I would like to thank: Ming Thein, Ted Gushue, Steve Hallock, Max Büsser, Tim Bent, George Glasgow Jr., Eric Wind, Kari Voutilainen, Sheena Lawrick, Bob Isaac, Dan Killian, Melise Gramm, and Erik Anders Lang. You have all been a joy to work with and I hope to collaborate with all of you again. Thank you.

Thank you to Maggie, Nancy, and Kristin—your support got me through the long days of drafting and editing.

Thank you to those of you who were early believers in the book: Sheena Lawrick, Maggie Searle, Dan Killian, Owen Zinamin, Thomas Miller, Darwin Hunt, Tom Saleh, Fred Bartels, Hilary Scott, Jack McAllister, Shane Quinlan, Matthew Downe, Alexander Fahmi, Gideon Searle, Kristin Searle, Nancy Searle, Robert Holman, Shannon Luloff, Jennifer Baryl, George Glasgow, Jr., Gordon DePuey, Sallie Griffith, Lorraine Schneider, GP Searle, Stacy Searle, Kathy Saitelbach, Caroline Kallman Joffe, Carter Hanson, Mike Pansky, Will Galvin, Kate McGuinness, Eric Koester, John Lee, and Nate Meierpolys. You provided the motivation I needed to finish this book. You have my most sincere thanks.

APPENDIX

All citations appear in the order in which they were cited by chapter.

1. Lee, Christine, Evren Esen, and Samantha DiNicola. "Executive Summary: Employee Job Satisfaction and Engagement: The Doors of Opportunity Are Open." Alexandria: Society for Human Resource Management, 2017. https://www.shrm.org/hr-today/trends-and-forecasting/research-and-surveys/Documents/2017-Employee-Job-Satisfaction-and-Engagement-Executive-Summary.pdf

2. Anderer, John. "Hindsight Is 20/20: 4 Out Of 10 Adults Regret Their Life Choices." Study Finds. Remember A Charity, July 23, 2019. https://www.studyfinds.org/hindsight-is-20-20-four-out-of-ten-adults-regret-their-life-choices/.

3. *SIHH2019: You Never Lose: You Win – Or You Learn / by MB&F. YouTube.* MB&F, 2019. https://www.youtube.com/watch?v=M9Pqi-QMoQw&t=1812s.

4. Rembach, Jim. "Innovation Secret Discovered at NASA." Beyond Morale: The Fearless Pursuit to Engage, October 31, 2016. https://www.beyondmorale.com/innovation-secret-discovered/.

5. Engels, Coert. "We Are Born Creative Geniuses and the Education System Dumbs Us down, According to NASA Scientists." Ideapod, 2018. https://ideapod.com/born-creative-geniuses-education-system-dumbs-us-according-nasa-scientists/.

6. *The Failure of Success.* Dr. George Land. *YouTube.* TEDx, 2011. https://www.youtube.com/watch?v=ZfKMq-rYtnc&t=323s.

7. "Episode #10.19." Episode. *Shark Tank.* Culver City, California: ABC, April 14, 2019.

8. Personal Journals, Todd Searle, 2015

9. Vint, Larry A. "Fresh Thinking Drives Creativity & Innovation." *QUICK - Journal of the Queensland Society for Information Technology in Education* 2005, no. 94 (2005): 20–22. https://research-repository.griffith.edu.au/bitstream/handle/10072/7880/33187_1.pdf?sequence=1&isAllowed=y.

10. Charron, Phil. "Divergent Thinking vs Convergent Thinking." Think Company. Think Company, March 12, 2019. https://www.thinkcompany.com/2011/10/divergent-thinking-vs-convergent-thinking/.

11. Moulton, Carly, and Dave Cosgrave. "Second Annual Self-Employment Report." FreshBooks. FreshBooks Cloud Accounting, April 2018. https://www.freshbooks.com/wp-content/uploads/2018/04/2018selfemploymentreport.pdf.

12. Cumberland, Dan. "The Psychology of Regret and How to Overcome It." The Meaning Movement, June 20, 2016. https://www.themeaningmovement.com/psychology-of-regret/.

13. Zeelenberg, Marcel, Wilco W. van Dijk, Anthony S.R. Manstead, and Joop van de Pligt. "On Bad Decisions and Disconfirmed Expectancies: The Psychology of Regret and Disappointment." *Cognition and Emotion* 14, no. 4 (2000): 521–41. https://doi.org/10.1080/026999300402781.

14. Shimanoff, Susan B. "Commonly Named Emotions in Everyday Conversations." *Perceptual and Motor Skills* 58, no. 2 (April 1984): 514–14. https://doi.org/10.2466/pms.1984.58.2.514.

15. Zeelenberg, Marcel, Wilco W. van Dijk, Antony S.R. Manstead, and Joop can der Pligt. "The Experience of Regret and Disappointment." *Cognition and Emotion* 12, no. 2 (1998): 221–30. https://doi.org/10.1080/026999398379727.

16. Saffrey, Colleen, Amy Summerville, and Neal J. Roese. "Praise for Regret: People Value Regret above Other Negative Emotions." *Motivation and Emotion* 32, no. 1 (2008): 46–54. https://doi.org/10.1007/s11031-008-9082-4.

17. Gushue, Ted [@tedgushue]. (2019, July 5). I'm Stuck in a Car for 5 hours. What do you want to know? Retrieved from: https://www.instagram.com/stories/highlights/18049860619164378/

18. Erik Anders Lang, "Ep 97: Erik Discusses How he Got Into Making Golf Content, A Round with a New Golfer and How Nothing in Life is Personal," Erik Anders Lang Show, January 21, 2019. Los Angeles, CA, Podcast, 01:01:49, https://open.spotify.com/episode/4i7M339FSgCRZsLeiSyArf?si=htXCuLAPQDCvmqimzmbpDw

19. Maximilian Büsser and Stephen Pulvirent, "Hodinkee Radio Episode 26: Maximilian Büsser," Hodinkee Radio Podcast, January 7, 2019, New York City, NY, podcast, 01:08:48, https://www.hodinkee.com/articles/hodinkee-radio-episode-26-maximilian-busser

20. Author Interview with Maximilian Büsser, July 8, 2019

21. Ellen Bennett and David Haber, "The Nitty-Gritty Podcast: Hedley & Bennett," Podcast, July 25, 2017, New York City, NY, Podcast, 1:04:17, https://soundcloud.com/bond-street-186109457/ellen-bennett-hedley-bennett

22. Greg McKeown and Tim Ferriss, "Greg McKeown – How to Master Essentialism (#355)," The Tim Ferriss Show, January 9, 2019, San Francisco, CA, podcast, 01:37:31, https://tim.blog/2019/01/09/greg-mckeown-essentialism/

23. Cal Newport, "About Me," Cal Newport, accessed September 2019, http://www.calnewport.com/about/.

24. Cal Newport, "Cal Newport – Deep Work, Digital Minimalism, and the Key to a Happy Retirement," Financial Independence Podcast, March 5, 2019, podcast, 49:16, https://podcasts.apple.com/us/podcast/cal-newport-deep-work-digital-minimalism-key-to-happy/id540593710?i=1000431124693

25. Thompson, John [John Thompson]. December, 2019. Response to LinkedIn Post regarding John's new book and his writing process. Retrieved from: https://www.linkedin.com/feed/update/urn:li:activity:6611738158793056256?commentUrn=urn%3Ali%3Acomment%3A%28activity%3A6611738158793056256%2C6611739368564543488%29&replyUrn=urn%3Ali%3Acomment%3A%28activity3A6611738158793056256%2C6611963792005885952%29

26. Hallock, Stephen [Steve Hallock]. December, 2019. LinkedIn Profile. Retrieved from: https://www.linkedin.com/in/stephenhallock/

27. Hallock, Steve. "About Me." TickTocking. Accessed August 2019. http://ticktocking.com/about/.

28. Maximilian Büsser, email to the author, July 28, 2019.

29. Oppezzo, Marily, and Daniel L. Schwartz. "Give Your Ideas Some Legs: The Positive Effect of Walking on Creative Thinking." *Journal of Experimental Psychology: Learning, Memory, and Cognition* 40, no. 4 (2014): 1142–52. https://doi.org/10.1037/a0036577.

30. Beres, Derek. "How Does the Brain-Body Connection Affect Creativity?" Big Think. Big Think, January 30, 2019. https://bigthink.com/21st-century-spirituality/walking-and-creativity.

31. Colzato, Lorenza S, Ayca Ozturk, and Bernhard Hommel. "Meditate to Create: The Impact of Focused-Attention and Open-Monitoring Training on Convergent and Divergent Thinking." Frontiers in Psychology. Leiden University, Leiden, Netherlands, March 30, 2012. https://www.frontiersin.org/articles/10.3389/fpsyg.2012.00116/full.

32. Hof, Isabelle. "The Wim Hof Method Explained." Translated by Claire van den Bergh. Wim Hof Method. Enahm Hof / Innerfire, June 2015. https://explore.wimhofmethod.com/wp-content/uploads/ebook-the-wim-hof-method-explained-EN.pdf.

33. McEvoy, Benjamin. "How Writers Can Improve Their Writing With The Wim Hof Method (Review)." Benjamin McEvoy, August 9, 2018. https://benjaminmcevoy.com/writers-can-improve-writing-wim-hof-method-review/.

34. Ming Thein, in-person meeting with the author, September 3, 2019

35. Ted Gushue and Stephen Pulvirent, "Hodinkee Radio Episode 15: Ted Gushue," Hodinkee Radio Podcast, October 15, 2018, New York City, NY, podcast, 01:07:44, https://www.hodinkee.com/articles/hodinkee-radio-episode-15-ted-gushue

36. Coon, J. Thompson, K. Boddy, K. Stein, R. Whear, J. Barton, and M. H. Depledge. "Does Participating in Physical Activity in Outdoor Natural Environments Have a Greater Effect on Physical and Mental Wellbeing than Physical Activity Indoors? A Systematic Review." *Environmental Science & Technology* 45, no. 5 (February 3, 2011): 1761–72. https://doi.org/10.1021/es102947t.

37. Singer, Michael A. "The Surrender Experiment." Essay. In *The Surrender Experiment*, 159–59. New York: Random House, 2015.

38. Chris Grainger and Jeremy Kirkland, "Chris Grainger: CEO of IWC," BLAMO! Podcast, July 22, 2019, 43:51, https://blamopod.com/blamo-podcast/2019/7/22/chris-grainger

39. Bent, Tim. "About." Bentleys Antique Shop London. Accessed August 2019. http://bentleyslondon.com/about/#theshop.

40. Merle, Andrew. "Why Curiosity Is The Key To Breakthrough Creativity." HuffPost. HuffPost, December 7, 2017. https://www.huffpost.com/entry/why-curiosity-is-the-key-_b_10764428?guce_referrer=aHR0cHM6Ly93d3cuZ29vZ2xlLmNvbS8&guce_referrer_sig=AQAAABNf80w_65Cw_AcaE8URTX16Hxl54ihJxgfTOTSV-LwYBqkUvs1unES2EUJD1IykeK_kg-goVTVgbbuxUrBhg79sw2Nz8YOVgeS8Bb99F9zQq1Xm2QJAcq2bQd-tubpieUA_9TOE7ndDo8misOjFFc8UnmYipfu7Rxa29vuglIWh&guccounter=2.

41. Amy Tan, *Where Does Creativity Hide?* TED2008. TED, 2008. https://www.ted.com/talks/amy_tan_where_does_creativity_hide?language=en.

42. Chamorro-Premuzic, Tomas. "Curiosity Is as Important as Intelligence." Harvard Business Review, November 5, 2014. https://hbr.org/2014/08/curiosity-is-as-important-as-intelligence.-+9*

ADDITIONAL SOURCES

1. Akay, Esin. "George Land's Creativity Test." L.I.F.E. Learning is Fun Everyday, January 16, 2015. https://esinakay.wordpress.com/tag/george-lands-creativity-test/.

2. Clear, James. "Debunking the Eureka Moment: Creative Thinking Is a Process." James Clear, June 12, 2018. https://jamesclear.com/creative-thinking.

3. Clear, James. "How to Master Creativity and Uncover Your Creative Genius." James Clear. Accessed July 2019. https://jamesclear.com/creativity.

4. Fritscher, Lisa. "Understanding the Dynamics of a Fear Response." Verywell Mind. Verywell Mind, September 14, 2019. https://www.verywellmind.com/the-psychology-of-fear-2671696.

5. Gilbert, Elizabeth. *Your Elusive Creative Genius. TED*. TED, 2009. https://www.ted.com/talks/elizabeth_gilbert_on_genius?language=en.

6. Kim, KH. "The Creativity Crisis: It's Getting Worse." Idea to Value, April 28, 2017. https://www.ideatovalue.com/crea/khkim/2017/04/creativity-crisis-getting-worse/.

7. MacLellan, Lila. "A New Study on the Psychology of Persistent Regrets Can Teach You How to Live Now." Quartz at Work. Quartz, June 17, 2018. https://qz.com/work/1298110/a-new-study-on-the-psychology-of-persistent-regrets-can-teach-you-how-to-live-now/.

8. 8. Merkovich, Aleks. "15 Entrepreneurship Statistics You Should Know." Fit Small Business. Fit Small Business, March 25, 2019. https://fitsmallbusiness.com/entrepreneurship-statistics/.

9. Nascimento, Gavin. "Study Shows We Are Born Creative Geniuses But The 'Education' System Dumbs Us Down?" A New Kind Of Human, May 24, 2019. https://anewkindofhuman.com/creative-genius-divergent-thinking-test/.

10. Pferdt, Frederik, and Tim Brown. "This Is the Way Google & IDEO Foster Creativity." IDEO U. IDEO U, August 30, 2017. https://www.ideou.com/blogs/inspiration/how-google-fosters-creativity-innovation.

11. Shankus, Evelyn. "Strategies of Divergent Thinking." Divergent Thinking. University of Washington. Accessed August 2019. https://faculty.washington.edu/ezent/imdt.htm.

12. Venkatraman, Rohini. "You're 96 Percent Less Creative Than You Were as a Child. Here's How to Reverse That." Inc.com. Inc., January 18, 2018. https://www.inc.com/rohini-venkatraman/4-ways-to-get-back-creativity-you-had-as-a-kid.html.

Made in the USA
Monee, IL
26 April 2020